How to Use This Book

Look for these special features in this book:

SIDEBARS, **CHARTS**, **GRAPHS**, and original **MAPS** expand your understanding of what's being discussed—and also make useful sources for classroom reports.

FAQs answer common **F**requently **A**sked **Q**uestions about people, places, and things.

WOW FACTORS offer "Who knew?" facts to keep you thinking.

TRAVEL GUIDE gives you tips on exploring the state—either in person or right from your chair!

PROJECT ROOM provides fun ideas for school assignments and incredible research projects. Plus, there's a guide to primary sources—what they are and how to cite them.

Please note: All statistics are as up-to-date as possible at the time of publication.

Consultants: Sarah Chadima, Geologist, South Dakota Geological Survey; Herbert Hoover, Professor Emeritus, University of South Dakota; William Loren Katz

Book production by The Design Lab

Library of Congress Cataloging-in-Publication Data
Burgan, Michael.
 South Dakota / by Michael Burgan.
   p. cm.—(America the beautiful. Third series)
Includes bibliographical references and index.
ISBN-13: 978-0-531-18503-2
ISBN-10: 0-531-18503-6
1. South Dakota—Juvenile literature. I. Title. II. Series.
F651.3.B87 2009
978.3—dc22   2008002299

1 2 3 4 5 6 7 8 9 10 R 19 18 17 16 15 14 13 12 11 10

AMERICA ★ THE ★ BEAUTIFUL

South Dakota

BY MICHAEL BURGAN

Third Series

Children's Press®
An Imprint of Scholastic Inc.
New York ★ Toronto ★ London ★ Auckland ★ Sydney
Mexico City ★ New Delhi ★ Hong Kong
Danbury, Connecticut

CONTENTS

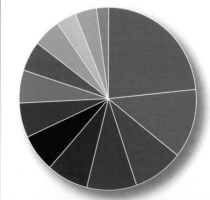

NORTH DAKOTA

Fort Sisseton
State Historical Park

Motorcycle
Museum &
Hall of Fame

Grand

Moreau

Missouri

ABERDEEN

WATERTOWN

South Dakota Air
and Space Museum

Great Lake
Dahe

Plains

South Dakota
Art Museum

Big Sioux

Black Hills
National
Forest

Cheyenne

SOUTH DAKOTA

James

PIERRE

South Dakota
State Capitol

RAPID CITY

Mount
Rushmore

Great Plains Zoo

White

SIOUX FALLS

Custer
State Park

Badlands
National Park

CHAMBERLAIN

Akta Lakota
Museum &
Cultural Center

Missouri

Jewel Cave
National Monument

Sitting Bull and
Sacagawea Monuments

South Dakota
Hall of Fame

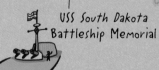

YANKTON

USS South Dakota
Battleship Memorial

NEBRASKA

0   40
Miles

Welcome to South Dakota!

HOW DID SOUTH DAKOTA GET ITS NAME?

Almost 300 years ago, a group of Native Americans headed west out of Minnesota searching for new hunting grounds. In their language, the word for "friend" was *koda* or *kola*. Some of these people called themselves Dakota, meaning "alliance of friends." Over time, European fur traders and explorers came to the native lands, located along the Missouri River and other nearby waterways. In 1861, the United States named this region the Dakota Territory. Twenty-eight years later, two states were formed from the territory: North Dakota and South Dakota.

SOUTH DAKOTA

8

READ
ABOUT

Badlands National
Park at sunset

CHAPTER ONE

LAND

★

SOUTH DAKOTA HAS BEEN CALLED "THE LAND OF INFINITE VARIETY." Infinite, or limitless, may not be completely accurate. Still, with its sprawling, flat plains, rolling hills, broad river valleys, and majestic mountains, South Dakota boasts a wide range of natural beauty. South Dakota is the 17th-largest state, with a total area of 77,117 square miles (199,732 square kilometers). Its highest point is 7,242 feet (2,207 meters) at Harney Peak in the Black Hills. Its lowest spot is 966 feet (294 m) at Big Stone Lake, in the northeast corner of the state.

FAQ

Q: WHAT IS THE LARGEST FOSSIL EVER FOUND IN SOUTH DAKOTA?

A: In 1990, explorer Sue Hendrickson was looking for dinosaur bones in the Black Hills of South Dakota. She uncovered the largest, most complete skeleton of a *T. rex* ever found. The *T. rex* skeleton, now called Sue, is on display at Chicago's Field Museum.

WORD TO KNOW

glaciers *slow-moving masses of ice*

ANCIENT WATER AND ICE

More than 300 million years ago, seas covered most of what is now the central United States, including South Dakota. At one time, huge sea turtles and other now-extinct water creatures lived in the region. Over millions of years, the seas receded and then returned several times. After the land was finally dry, dinosaurs and ancient mammals lived in today's South Dakota. These included *Tyrannosaurus rex*, one of the largest meat eaters ever to walk the earth. Fossils of these dinosaurs and other ancient creatures are still being uncovered in the state today.

About 2 million years ago, huge continental ice sheets began to drift southward over North America. These **glaciers** shaped the land of eastern South Dakota by crushing and scraping the land's surface in their path. The last glaciers melted away about 10,000 years

South Dakota Geo-Facts

Along with the state's geographical highlights, this chart ranks South Dakota's land, water, and total area compared to all other states.

Total area; rank . . . . . .77,117 square miles (199,732 sq km); 17th
Land; rank . . . . .75,885 square miles (196,541 sq km); 16th
Water; rank . . . . .1,232 square miles (3,191 sq km); 29th
Inland water; rank . . . . . 1,232 square miles (3,191 sq km); 16th
Geographic center . . . .Hughes, 8 miles (13 km) northeast of Pierre
Latitude . . . . 42°29'30" N to 45°56' N
Longitude . . . . .98°28'33" W to 104°3' W
Highest point . . . . .Harney Peak, 7,242 feet (2,207 m), in Pennington County
Lowest point . . . . Big Stone Lake, 966 feet (294 m), in Roberts County
Largest city . . . . Sioux Falls
Longest river . . . . .Missouri River

Source: U.S. Census Bureau

Rhode Island, the smallest U.S. state, could fit inside South Dakota 49 times.

ago, leaving sand, gravel, and clay behind. The melting ice also created lakes and rivers.

In western South Dakota, the land was further shaped by ancient oceans and **erosion**. Some of the rocks on the surface are made up of materials that once lay on ocean bottoms. In other areas, erosion has deposited and carved land out of rocks.

LAND REGIONS

South Dakota sits almost in the middle of the Great Plains, a mostly flat, grassy region that stretches from northern Mexico to the heart of Canada. In the United States, the Great Plains cuts through the center of the country, roughly halfway between the Rocky Mountains and the Mississippi River.

The landscape of South Dakota features three main regions: the Central Lowlands, the Great Plains, and the Black Hills.

A researcher works on a 25,000-year-old mammoth skeleton at Hot Springs.

WORD TO KNOW

erosion *the wearing away of land by water, ice, wind, and other factors*

South Dakota Topography

Use the color-coded elevation chart to see on the map South Dakota's high points (dark red to orange) and low points (green to dark green). Elevation is measured as the distance above or below sea level.

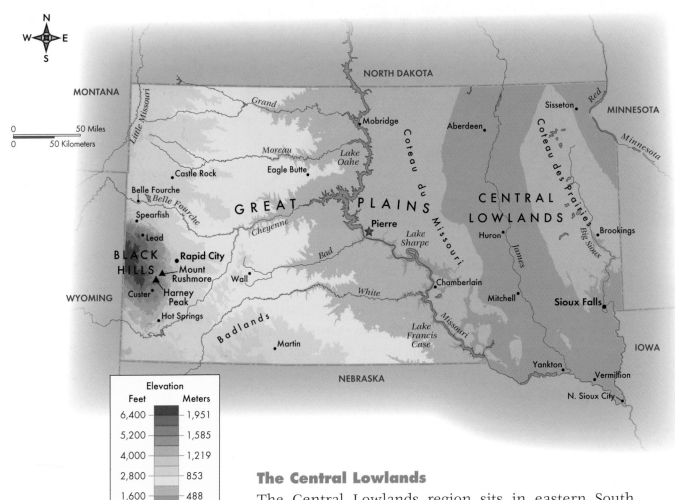

Elevation	
Feet	Meters
6,400	1,951
5,200	1,585
4,000	1,219
2,800	853
1,600	488

WORD TO KNOW

plateau *an elevated part of the earth with steep slopes*

The Central Lowlands

The Central Lowlands region sits in eastern South Dakota. A large part of the region is the James River Lowland, a low-lying plain. Another part of this region is actually a **plateau** that rises about 2,000 feet (610 m) above sea level. Called the Coteau des Prairies (French for "slope of the prairies"), this plateau is about 200 miles (322 km) long and 100 miles (161 km) wide. Hills

Horses grazing in Jones County, in the central part of the state

dot the Central Lowlands, an area that features some of the best farmland in the country.

The Great Plains

This region of South Dakota begins east of the Missouri River and stretches west, covering almost two-thirds of the state. It includes an interesting feature, the Missouri River Trench, where the land drops suddenly from a plateau to a narrow valley along the river. The Great Plains region is covered with grasslands that provide food for herds of cattle, sheep, and other grazing animals.

In the southwestern part of the Great Plains region is a dry stretch of land with deep canyons, towering spires, and flat-topped tables. The Sioux Indians called it *mako sica*—"land bad." Today, it is called the Badlands. The term *badlands* refers to any dry, heavily eroded land.

SEE IT HERE!

BADLANDS NATIONAL PARK

Ancient oceans helped form the layers of rock that make up the Badlands. Rivers and rain then eroded the soft layers of rock, shaping the steep, jagged cliffs called buttes. Even today, rain can cause a butte to fall to the ground. The U.S. government first recognized the unique beauty of the Badlands in 1929 and in 1978 made it into a national park. Within the park are fossils dating back more than 79 million years.

The Black Hills

Look at a map of the United States, and you'll see the Rocky Mountains cutting north to south across the western part of the country. To the east of this range are the Black Hills, which formed at almost the same time as the Rockies. These "hills," which reach more than 7,000 feet (2,100 m) high, have been called a mini version of the mighty Rockies. The mountains contain gold, lead, and other mineral resources.

From the air, the rocks of the Black Hills look very much like an oblong archery target. Rings of different rocks dip away from the center. The most dramatic ring on the outside of the target is called the Great Hogback. These series of steep slopes reminded early explorers of the ridges on the back of a razorback hog. At the Needles, another region in the Black Hills, rock climbers test their skills on the thin, sharp spires.

Hikers on Harney Peak in the Black Hills

THE MISSOURI AND OTHER RIVERS

On its way from Montana to the Mississippi River, the 2,341-mile-long (3,767 km) Missouri River flows through South Dakota. For much of its journey through the state, the Missouri River almost divides South Dakota in half, separating east and west. Then the river takes a turn east and forms part of the border between South Dakota and Nebraska. In the eastern half of the state, the major rivers flow north to south, including the James and the Big Sioux. West of the Missouri, the rivers flow primarily from west to east. These include the Grand, Moreau, Cheyenne, Bad, and White rivers.

CLIMATE

South Dakota has cold winters and warm summers. The southeast is the wettest part of the state. North of this region, less **precipitation** falls and the summers are a little shorter. In the west, the air tends to be drier. In the Black Hills, weather conditions change quickly, depending on elevation and location. On the whole, this is the coldest part of the state. South Dakota is generally very windy. Even on a sunny day, the constant stiff winds can make it hard to walk or open a car door.

In the spring and summer, thunderstorms and tornadoes are common in South Dakota.

In 1968, winds of up to 150 miles per hour (241 kph) blew through parts of eastern South Dakota for 20 minutes. That's as strong as an extremely damaging hurricane.

WORD TO KNOW

precipitation *all water that falls to the earth, including rain, sleet, hail, snow, dew, fog, or mist*

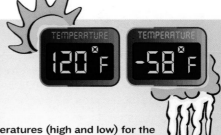

Weather Report

This chart shows record temperatures (high and low) for the state, as well as average temperatures (July and January) and average annual precipitation.

Record high temperature . . . . 120°F (49°C) at Gann Valley on July 5, 1936
Record low temperature . . . . –58°F (–50°C) at McIntosh on February 17, 1936
Average July temperature .72°F (22°C)
Average January temperature . . . . 22°F (–6°C)
Average yearly precipitation . . . . .16 inches (41 cm)

Source: National Climatic Data Center, NESDIS, NOAA, U.S. Department of Commerce

A bison roams a snow-covered plain in South Dakota.

The town of Lead holds the state record for annual snowfall. In 1997, it got 324 inches (823 centimeters)—that's 27 feet!

The winter brings snowstorms and, on average, three full-blown blizzards a year. In 1888, during one of the worst blizzards in the state's history, dozens of school-children died as they walked home from school and got caught in the storm.

PLANT LIFE

Vast grasslands once blanketed South Dakota. Prairie grass up to 6 feet (1.8 m) tall covered the southeastern corner of South Dakota. Farmland has since replaced much of this grass. The height of the prairie grass decreases as you move from east to west across the state. About two-thirds of the state, starting east of the Missouri River, is called the short- and mid-grass region. Cattle, sheep, and other livestock graze on blue grama and wheatgrass that grow there.

The state flower, the American pasque, grows all across the state, most commonly in the east. Prairie rose and goldenrod also brighten the plains.

Only about 4 percent of South Dakota's land is covered with trees. Nearly all of this woodland is located in the Black Hills. Many kinds of pines grow there, along with the Black Hills spruce—the state tree. Leaf-bearing trees are not as common as evergreens in South Dakota, but cottonwood, black walnut, and ash do grow in the state.

A prairie coneflower growing among horsemint in Wind Cave National Park

South Dakota National Park Areas

This map shows some of South Dakota's national parks, monuments, preserves, and other areas protected by the National Park Service.

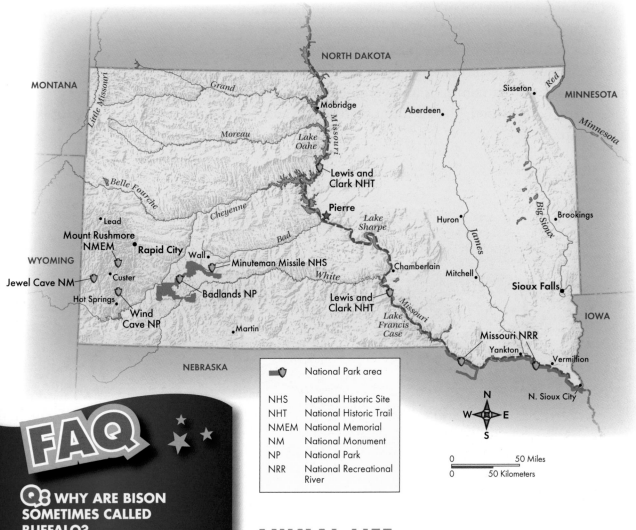

	National Park area
NHS	National Historic Site
NHT	National Historic Trail
NMEM	National Memorial
NM	National Monument
NP	National Park
NRR	National Recreational River

0   50 Miles
0   50 Kilometers

ANIMAL LIFE

A wide variety of wildlife live on South Dakota's prairies, plains, and mountains. Deer and pronghorn thrive, as do elk, mountain lions, and wolves. The coyote is the state animal, and sometimes South Dakota is called the Coyote State. Huge herds of bison, often called

ENDANGERED ANIMALS

South Dakotans are trying to protect animals in danger of becoming extinct. The Eskimo curlew and the majestic whooping crane are two birds in danger because they have lost their habitat. Fish on the state's **endangered** species list include the pallid sturgeon and the banded killifish. Two insects in danger are the American burying beetle and the Dakota skipper, a type of butterfly.

buffalo, once roamed the state, but their numbers fell sharply in the 19th century, and they almost became extinct. Today, bison herds again live on preserves in the west and on ranches across the state. Mountain goats and wild burros live in the Black Hills. Small mammals in the state include jackrabbits, prairie dogs, and squirrels.

Bald eagles nest in South Dakota each year. More common birds are pheasants, ducks, geese, hawks, owls, and finches. South Dakota has just one native poisonous snake—the prairie rattler. Most are found west of the Missouri River. In the state's lakes, rivers, and streams live fish such as walleye, bass, trout, and carp.

The whooping crane is an endangered species that is native to South Dakota.

WORD TO KNOW

endangered *at risk of becoming extinct*

Prairie dogs

WORD TO KNOW

shelterbelts *rows of trees that provide shelter from the wind*

In 2007, South Dakotans planted almost 2 million trees, including 535 miles (861 km) of farm shelterbelts.

These pronghorn fawns in Custer State Park are among many animals protected in South Dakota's natural areas.

HUMANS AND THE ENVIRONMENT

When European American settlers first came to South Dakota, they began to plow up the prairies to create farmland. By the 21st century, more than 40 percent of South Dakota's native prairie had disappeared. Wetlands have disappeared at almost the same rate. As these environments are lost, the plants and animals that live there find it hard to survive.

In recent years, South Dakotans have worked to save some of the remaining prairies and wetlands. Ranchers move livestock around from year to year, so the grass they graze on has a chance to regrow. As new buildings are constructed, developers set aside some land as wildlife habitat. Farmers plant grass and trees on the edges of their farms to provide new homes for animals of all kinds.

The rows of trees found along many South Dakota farms are called windbreaks, or **shelterbelts**. The trees

Modern wind turbines, shown near a wooden windmill, help generate energy in South Dakota.

LINDA M. HASSELSTROM: WRITER, RANCHER, ENVIRONMENTALIST

Linda Hasselstrom (1943–) grew up on a ranch in Hermosa, near the Black Hills. After graduating from the University of South Dakota, she left the state for a time before returning home to the family ranch. Her experiences on the ranch led her to write books and poems about life on the Great Plains. Living close to the land helped her realize how important it is to save the grasslands and the plants and animals that live there. For a time, Hasselstrom worked with environmental groups, but she decided writing was a more effective way to show others the need to preserve the Great Plains. She now operates a writing center on her ranch.

 Want to know more?
See www.windbreakhouse.com

help prevent the wind and water from carrying away the soil, keeping farmland healthy.

South Dakotans are also looking for ways to create energy that will not pollute the environment the way burning coal and oil do. The state's persistent wind may be one of its greatest resources because it can provide a clean source of power. In 2007, a California company announced plans to erect huge wind **turbines** in South Dakota. This "wind farm" would be the largest in the world. The state already has wind farms in McPherson and Brookings counties, and more are on the way.

WORD TO KNOW

turbines *machines for making power through the rotation of blades powered by wind, water, or steam*

READ ABOUT

Early hunters
crossing the
Bering Strait
from Asia

▲ **c. 10,000 BCE**
*Native people hunt
mammoths in what is
now South Dakota*

c. 500 CE
*Mound Builders
arrive in South
Dakota*

c. 1000
*Pre-Arikaras arrive
in the region*

CHAPTER TWO

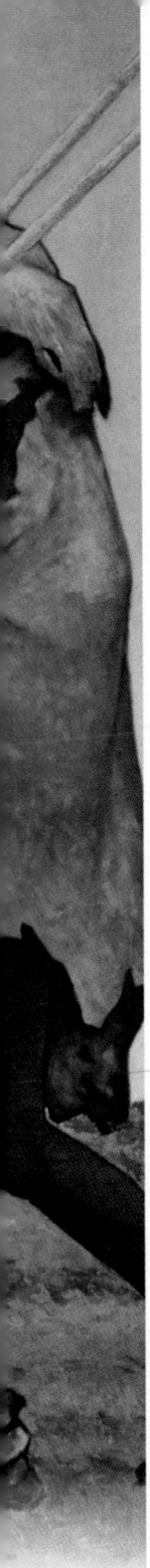

FIRST PEOPLE

★

SCIENTISTS BELIEVE THAT THE ANCESTORS OF THE FIRST SOUTH DAKOTANS TRAVELED TO NORTH AMERICA FROM ASIA. Some people may have walked over a land bridge that once connected what are now Russia and Alaska. Others may have come by boat. From their landing points, these first settlers spread out over North America.

Arikara pottery

c. 1600

Arikaras begin trading for European goods

mid-1700s

Sioux come to South Dakota from Minnesota

▲ **c. 1300–mid-1500s**

Arikaras arrive in South Dakota

In the area that is now South Dakota, early peoples hunted bison for food and clothing.

WORD TO KNOW

archaeologists *people who study the remains of past human societies*

EARLY HUNTERS AND GATHERERS

The first people to reach today's South Dakota used sharp, stone-tipped spears to kill prey such as mammoths and mastodons. The animals provided food, and hunters turned the bones into tools. On the Pine Ridge Indian Reservation in southwestern South Dakota, **archaeologists** have found evidence that early hunters killed mammoths there about 12,000 years ago.

During the next several thousand years, different groups of people came to South Dakota to hunt. They were nomadic, walking from place to place in search of game. By about 8000 BCE, mammoths and mastodons were extinct, and bison became the main food for people in today's South Dakota. People hunted bison both by spearing them and by chasing them off cliffs. They also killed smaller animals and gathered wild plants such as vegetables and berries.

FIRST VILLAGES

Around 500 CE, people from the south began to move into today's South Dakota. They are sometimes called the Mound Builders, because they buried their dead under huge mounds of earth. Later Mound Builders, called Mississippians, erected their most important buildings atop the mounds.

In South Dakota, Mound Builders settled in small villages along rivers such as the Big Sioux and the Missouri. They hunted, fished, and farmed, raising corn, squash, and beans.

PRE-ARIKARA

Starting around the year 1000, people now called Pre-Arikaras moved into South Dakota from Minnesota. They built much larger villages than the Mound Builders had, and they erected tall, wooden fences called palisades around their communities. The palisades were designed to keep out invading enemies. Pre-Arikaras made their homes, or lodges, out of a mixture of grass and clay. Wooden posts held up the ceilings, which were made of grass mats and branches. As many as 20 family members might have shared one lodge.

Pre-Arikaras regularly traded with other Native Americans. They obtained stones such as flint and quartz—which they used as arrow and spear points— most likely by trading extra food they had grown.

ARIKARA

The Arikara people moved into South Dakota between 1300 and the mid-1500s, settling along the Missouri and Grand rivers. Like Pre-Arikaras, they farmed and lived in earthen lodges. Sometimes they also used tipis, cone-shaped tents made with bison skins.

SEE IT HERE!

A VILLAGE FROM THE PAST

In 1910, a college student from Mitchell uncovered the remains of a village that was about 1,000 years old. Since then, archaeologists have worked at the site, learning more about the Native people who once lived there. Today, the dig site is the heart of the Mitchell Prehistoric Indian Village. A huge building covers the dig site where archaeologists continue to work. Visitors can see traces of the village. A separate museum contains a model of an earth lodge and provides details about the lives of Pre-Arikaras.

Arikara man

Native American Peoples
(Before European Contact)

This map shows the general area of Native American peoples before European settlers arrived.

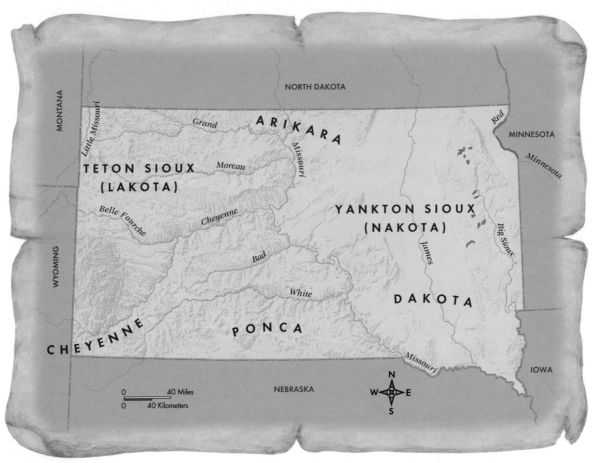

Corn was so central to Arikara life that the people sometimes called themselves "corn eaters."

In Arikara villages, women were the farmers. In addition to corn, squash, and beans, they also raised pumpkins and tobacco. They traded extra crops to the Lakota Sioux, Cheyenne, and other nations for animal hides and, later, horses. Starting around 1600, Arikaras also traded for goods from Europe, including metal pots and guns. The first European traders and explorers had come to North America in the early 16th century.

Members of the Dakota people, who
settled in the eastern part of the region

SIOUX

While Arikaras thrived in their villages, Native people
from Minnesota sometimes came to South Dakota to
hunt and fish. In the mid-18th century, they began settling in South Dakota. Ojibwa people called these communities *Nadowe Su*, which means "little rattle." The
name refers to the rattle of a rattlesnake. Eventually,
the name of the newcomers was shortened to Sioux.

The Sioux eventually divided into three main
groups: Dakota, Nakota, and Lakota. The Dakota people
settled in the southeastern part of South Dakota. They
included four groups: Mdewakantons, Wahpekutes,
Sissetons, and Wahpetons. To the northwest of them
lived the Nakota people, who were divided into Yanktons,
the Upper and Lower Yanktonais, and Assiniboines. In

In winter, Sioux hunters sometimes used snowshoes in their pursuit of bison.

To the Sioux, even a bison's stomach was useful. It was cleaned out and used as a sack to store and carry water.

western South Dakota, near the Black Hills, lived the Lakota people. They were divided into Oglalas, Brulés, Minneconjous, Sans Arcs, Two Kettles, Blackfoot Sioux, and Hunkpapas.

Sioux were expert hunters. Bison was their main prey, but they also hunted bear, elk, and deer. They used almost every part of the bison for their daily needs. They turned the hides into robes, shirts, belts, and tipi covers. They made tools from the bones, and the animals' horns served as cups and spoons. For hundreds of years, Sioux hunted bison on foot, but in the mid-1700s, they obtained horses from other Native American nations, which made hunting easier.

There were differences in the ways the three main groups lived. Dakotas had large lodges where some people lived while raising corn or gathering nuts and berries. The majority of Nakotas lived in permanent villages year-round. Lakotas were the most nomadic of the Sioux nations, often following herds of bison across the plains. In winter, they settled in camps, where they prepared for the next hunting season. Hunters from all groups lived in tipis as they traveled.

In Sioux society, men spent most of their time hunting game, trading with other tribes, or waging war. Men, especially Lakota men, were expert riders and skilled with a bow and arrow. In battle, Sioux fighters valued bravery and skill, not killing the enemy. A warrior would ride up and touch an opponent with a special stick. This act was called counting coup, and warriors wore feathers that showed how many coup they had counted.

Sioux women took charge of the family and the camps. They owned a family's tipi and set it up after each move. Women also butchered bison for their meat and tanned their hides so they could be used for clothing. Sioux women raised crops and gathered nuts, seeds, and berries for meals.

ELLA DELORIA: ANTHROPOLOGIST

In her Yankton Sioux family, Ella Deloria (1889–1971) was called Apetu Waste Win—"Beautiful Day Woman." Deloria left her Yankton reservation and spent time with the Lakota before becoming an **anthropologist**. As part of her work, she visited South Dakota reservations and gathered stories about Sioux history. That research was the core of her 1932 book Dakota Texts, which explains Sioux culture and language to the outside world. Throughout her career, she met her goal of making "the Dakota people understandable, as human beings, to the white people who dealt with them."

? **Want to know more?** See www.mnsu.edu/emuseum/information/biography/abcde/deloria_ella_cara.html

WORD TO KNOW

anthropologist *a person who studies the development of human cultures*

FAQ

Q: WHAT WERE WINTER COUNTS?

A: A winter count served as the Lakota's visual calendar and history book. It was made of animal hides with pictures drawn on them. Each year, the calendar's keeper drew an image that represented important events from the past year.

Picture Yourself...

Growing Up in a Lakota Camp

As a child, you stayed close to your mother as she searched for food and set up the family tipi. But now you are older. You are expected to search for food, too, and to gather firewood. If you are a boy, at about age 12 or 13 you go with your father and other men to learn the skills of a warrior. You've been riding and racing horses for several years already, and you've learned to shoot a bow and arrow. If you are a girl, you learn how to skin bison, sew, and set up tipis.

Meat drying outside tipis on the plains

As they went about their daily lives, Sioux felt the presence of many spirits. Some spirits helped humans, while others represented evil. To Sioux, the universe was the creation of Wakan Tanka Tunkasila, the Great (or Holy) Spirit, Grandfather. All people, animals, and plants were connected through the creator. Even rocks and other nonliving things were *wakan*, meaning "holy."

Lakotas honored Wakan Tanka Tunkasila and other spirits. They also believed certain animals had special powers or offered special services to humans. Bison, for example, were sacred because they provided everything the Sioux needed to live. Bison skulls were used in some religious ceremonies. Bears were thought to show Lakotas which roots could be used to cure illnesses.

To stay in touch with the spirit world, the Sioux relied on medicine men, who were thought to have been born knowing the nature of what was sacred. Learning from the medicine men who came before them, Sioux gained the skills to understand the spirits and what they wanted humans to do.

The vision quest was a key part of a Sioux's spiritual life. On a vision quest, a person—usually a man—

MODERN-DAY MEDICINE MAN

In the 19th and 20th centuries, the U.S. government tried to destroy the Sioux's ancient spiritual beliefs and practices. But some medicine men, such as Wallace Black Elk (1921–2004) secretly learned the old ways. Black Elk grew up on the Rosebud Reservation, where he spent time with a medicine man named Nicholas Black Elk. Once Wallace Black Elk mastered these skills, he shared Lakota beliefs in a book, interviews, and lectures. He pushed for a law, passed in 1978, that gave all Native Americans the freedom to follow their traditional spiritual practices. He believed non-Sioux could also benefit from learning the ancient wisdom of his people.

A portrait of Blue Medicine, a medicine man of the eastern Dakotas, by painter George Catlin

went out alone onto a high hill for up to four days. He went without food and water, waiting for the spirits to send a message. The spirit might appear in the form of an animal or bird. Once the person had a vision, he returned home and discussed what he had seen or heard with a medicine man, who helped him understand it. With the wisdom gained from vision quests, Sioux believed they would lead better lives.

READ ABOUT

Trappers
setting out for
a beaver hunt

1700s
A smallpox epidemic
kills thousands of
Arikaras

1743 ▲
The La Vérendrye
brothers are the first
known European
explorers in South
Dakota

1804
The Lewis and
Clark expedition
travels through South
Dakota on the way to
the Pacific Ocean

CHAPTER THREE

EXPLORATION AND SETTLEMENT

★

IN THE 17TH CENTURY, FRENCH FUR TRADERS AND TRAPPERS WORKED NEAR THE UPPER MISSISSIPPI RIVER AND THE GREAT LAKES. Through trade, their goods reached the Arikara people of South Dakota. Then, starting early in the 18th century, French traders themselves came to South Dakota, and European settlement slowly followed.

▲ **early 1800s**
The fur trade thrives in South Dakota

1857
Sioux Falls, the first permanent European American town in South Dakota, is founded

1861
The United States creates the Dakota Territory

European Exploration of South Dakota

The colored arrows on this map show the routes taken by explorers between 1743 and 1806.

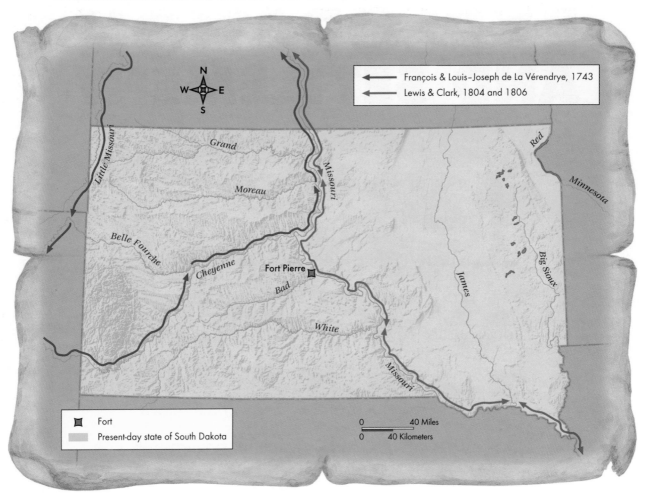

François & Louis-Joseph de La Vérendrye, 1743

Lewis & Clark, 1804 and 1806

Fort

Present-day state of South Dakota

0 — 40 Miles
0 — 40 Kilometers

EUROPEANS ARRIVE

French trappers working along the Minnesota River might have been the first Europeans to enter South Dakota. By 1701, the French had made a map of the region around the Big Sioux River. The first documented proof of Europeans in South Dakota came in 1743. Two French Canadian brothers, Louis-Joseph and François de La Vérendrye, led a small party south from what

The La Vérendrye brothers explored the region in 1743.

is now Canada. Along the way, they buried two metal plates that their father had made in Quebec, Canada. The dates and the names of several of the explorers were scratched into the metal. The plates were discovered in the 20th century.

For decades after the La Vérendrye explorations, few Europeans came to South Dakota. Still, the presence of Europeans in North America was already spelling disaster for some Native people in today's South Dakota. During the 18th century, the Arikara population reached a height of about 30,000. But diseases, such as smallpox, that Europeans brought with them to North America began to have a deadly effect. The Arikara Nation and

A Labrador retriever named Ben helped uncover some of South Dakota's history—he found one of the La Vérendrye plates in 1995.

WORD TO KNOW

allies *people who are on the same side in a conflict*

WORD TO KNOW

expedition *a trip for the purpose of exploration*

neighboring groups had no natural defenses against these illnesses. Arikaras died by the thousands.

After the British defeated the French and their Indian **allies** in the French and Indian War (1754–1763), France lost most of its colonial lands in North America to Great Britain. But the British focused on their existing trade in Canada instead of exploring lands farther west. The Revolutionary War between Great Britain and the 13 American colonies further cut down travel and trade in the west.

At the end of the American Revolution in 1783, South Dakota was part of the vast Louisiana Territory, which stretched west from the Mississippi River all the way to the Rocky Mountains. Spain controlled this territory, though most of the settlers were French. The British, however, were entering the Dakotas to trade with Native people. Americans also eyed these western lands. In 1793, the Spanish formed the Missouri Company, based in St. Louis, to explore South Dakota. The Spanish were interested in trading with Native Americans and keeping the British out.

The next year, a Missouri Company **expedition** led by Jean Baptiste Truteau entered South Dakota. During this trip, Truteau built the first known European building in South Dakota, a small cabin near what is now Fort Randall. In 1800, a St. Louis trader named Régis Loisel built a larger fort south of present-day Pierre. Soon, however, the Spanish and French in Louisiana would find themselves residents of the United States.

LEWIS AND CLARK

In 1800, Spain secretly gave Louisiana to France, which had controlled that territory for most of the 18th century. Then in 1803, France sold Louisiana to the United

States for $15 million, or about four cents an acre (0.4 ha). President Thomas Jefferson recruited Meriwether Lewis and William Clark to lead an expedition through the new U.S. lands. Jefferson hoped to build good relations with Native American nations in the region and to find a water route to the Pacific.

The Lewis and Clark expedition began traveling up the Missouri River from St. Louis, Missouri, on May 14, 1804. They passed through South Dakota, and by winter reached today's North Dakota, where they met Sacagawea, a young Shoshone woman who became their leading interpreter. She was assisted by York, an enslaved African who had been Clark's companion since childhood. The members of the expedition gave Sacagawea and York the right to vote on expedition matters as a reward for their services and sacrifices.

The members of the expedition also met Arikaras, Yanktons, Yanktonais, and Lakotas. The expedition members got along well with Arikaras. But Lakotas along the Missouri near today's Pierre, South Dakota, would not let the expedition

WOW

The Louisiana Purchase nearly doubled the size of the United States. All or parts of 15 states were carved out of the Louisiana Territory, including South Dakota.

Louisiana Purchase

This map shows the area (in yellow) that made up the Louisiana Purchase and the present-day state of South Dakota (in orange).

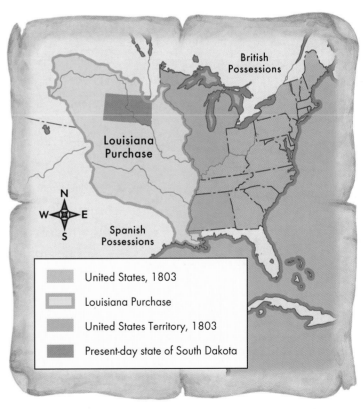

British Possessions

Louisiana Purchase

N
W E
S

Spanish Possessions

- United States, 1803
- Louisiana Purchase
- United States Territory, 1803
- Present-day state of South Dakota

MINI-BIO

YORK: EXPLORING THE WEST

The Lewis and Clark expedition included one African American, an enslaved man named York (c. 1770–c. 1831). He was the first African American known to set foot in South Dakota. York was an excellent hunter and fisher, picked up languages quickly, and served as an ambassador of goodwill with the Native Americans. He also cooked, helped build forts, and scouted trails. Some historians believe that Clark gave York his freedom sometime after 1815 and that he went into business for himself, carrying goods for others in a horse-drawn wagon.

❓ **Want to know more?** See www.lewisandclarktrail. com/york.htm

Sacagawea guiding the Lewis and Clark expedition

WOW

In South Dakota, Lewis and Clark captured a prairie dog and black-billed magpies and sent them back to President Jefferson in Washington, D.C.

pass without paying a toll, and Lewis and Clark feared violence would break out. At first, Lewis and Clark refused to pay, but they finally offered a gift of tobacco.

The expedition continued on and reached the Pacific Ocean in 1805. On the return trip to St. Louis, they once again passed through South Dakota's Lakota and Nakota villages. The expedition finally ended in September 1806.

TRADERS AND TRAPPERS

The Lewis and Clark expedition turned many American eyes toward the west. Foreigners were also interested in the wealth the Louisiana Territory held. In South

Dakota, British, French, and Spanish traders joined Americans in the search for fur. Beaver was especially prized, as it was used in clothing in both the United States and Europe. Bison, deer, mink, and otter were also hunted for their skins and fur.

During the first decades of the 19th century, several large trading companies operated in South Dakota, the most important led by Pierre Chouteau Jr. The companies traded metal tools, glass beads, guns, and other items to Native American trappers who brought their furs to the trading posts. Some trading posts were just small cabins, but Fort Pierre, which Chouteau built, was a major post, with palisade walls 15 feet (4.6 m) high and cannons defending it.

In 1831, Chouteau used a steamboat to bring goods to the region and take furs back to St. Louis. Steamboats could travel faster and carry more goods than boats that needed poles or oars.

Fort Pierre on the Upper Missouri River

SEE IT HERE!

SPIRIT MOUND

Historians are not sure about all the spots along the Missouri River where Lewis and Clark came ashore. But the explorers definitely reached South Dakota's Spirit Mound, 6 miles (10 km) north of Vermillion. Native people told the expedition that beings just 18 inches (46 cm) tall, with large heads, lived on the hill. Lewis, Clark, and several others walked four hours through intense summer heat to reach the hill. They didn't see any little people, but from the top they did see herds of bison. Today, Spirit Mound is a state park, and you can retrace the steps of the explorers to the top of the hill.

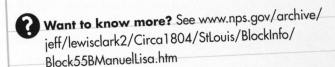

MANUEL LISA: SUCCESSFUL TRADER

When Lewis and Clark prepared for their mission, Manuel Lisa (1772–1820) helped supply them. Lisa, whose parents were Spanish, was born in New Orleans, Louisiana. He became a successful merchant in St. Louis, and in 1809, he and several other men formed the Missouri Fur Company. This company controlled the fur trade in South Dakota for several years, and Lisa made many trips to the region. He got along well with Native Americans, and he briefly worked for the U.S. government, handling Indian relations. More than any other person, he opened up trade along the Upper Missouri River.

? **Want to know more?** See www.nps.gov/archive/jeff/lewisclark2/Circa1804/StLouis/BlockInfo/Block55BManuelLisa.htm

Artist George Catlin

WORDS TO KNOW

naturalist *a person who studies natural history*

missionary *a person who tries to convert others to a religion*

In 1830, traders working along the Upper Missouri River sent 26,000 bison robes and 25,000 pounds (11,300 kilograms) of beaver fur to St. Louis.

Traders were not the only people who traveled through South Dakota. **Naturalist** John James Audubon visited the region to study birds and other wildlife, while artist George Catlin painted scenes of Sioux life. John C. Frémont led an expedition that explored lakes in eastern South Dakota. Later, he would run for president. Priests and ministers also came to the region. A Belgian **missionary** named Pierre-Jean De Smet spent time trying to convert Nakota Sioux to Christianity.

LOSING THEIR LAND

Native Americans along the Missouri River and in the Great Plains received many goods by trading with

Americans and Europeans. But at times, some fought with traders and explorers who entered their lands. In 1823, Arikaras attacked two boats traveling up the Missouri River, and the U.S. military sent troops to threaten the Arikaras. The U.S. forces were joined by hundreds of Sioux, the Arikaras' traditional enemies. The Arikara people escaped, but by the mid-1800s, they had moved north, out of South Dakota.

In 1825, the U.S. government signed peace treaties with various Sioux groups. In the next few decades, however, more Americans moved west onto the Great Plains or passed through on their way to California and Oregon. The U.S. government wanted to move Native peoples to reservations. This would open Indian land to settlement and hopefully keep the peace.

In 1851, Lakotas and other Plains Indians met with U.S. officials at Fort Laramie, Wyoming. They agreed not to attack settlers heading west and to leave certain areas, though they would not go to reservations. In return, the U.S. officials promised to give the Indians goods worth $50,000 every year.

Trouble near Fort Laramie, however, soon led to an increased military presence in South Dakota. In 1854, a Brulé Lakota man killed a cow belonging to white settlers. Troops rode in, violence broke out, and Brulés killed all the U.S. soldiers.

Picture Yourself . . .

at Fort Laramie

You are a Lakota, and for several years you have seen a stream of white settlers venture across your land. You and some of your people decide to go to Fort Laramie, Wyoming, to meet with U.S. representatives. When you arrive, you see a vast camp of tipis. Ten thousand Plains Indians have gathered for the talks. Before the meeting begins, you dance and eat. A ceremonial cannon shot greets you and the others at the start of the talks. You listen as Indian leaders and U.S. officials speak of the need for peaceful relations. You watch as the leaders pass around a calumet, a ceremonial pipe that is a sign of their desire for peace. The leaders sign the treaty, and you leave the meeting hoping that the promises of peaceful relations will last.

The next year, the U.S. government bought Fort Pierre to use as a military base. The fort was in bad shape, so in 1856, Fort Randall was built on the west side of the Missouri River, near the present-day South Dakota–Nebraska border. When the fort was complete, about 500 soldiers could live there.

In 1858, Yankton Sioux signed a treaty with the U.S. government. The Yankton people believed that the flood of white settlers into South Dakota could not be stopped. They agreed to surrender more than 11 million acres (4.4 million hectares) of land and move to a reservation in exchange for $1.6 million.

GROWING SETTLEMENTS

European explorers and Americans from other areas had long traded furs at South Dakota forts, but for many years no permanent European-American town was founded in the region. Then in 1857, settlers from Iowa and Minnesota created the town of Sioux Falls at a large waterfall along the Big Sioux River. The first settlers built a fort, and 17 men spent the winter there. In 1859, the town of Yankton grew up on lands that Yankton Sioux had sold to the United States.

MINI-BIO

JOHN BLAIR SMITH TODD: VOICE FOR DAKOTA

In 1855, John Blair Smith Todd (1814–1872) came to South Dakota as a U.S. Army officer. When he left the military the next year, he began working as a trader at Fort Randall. With his business partners, Todd helped convince the Yankton Sioux to sell their land to the U.S. government. He then helped found the city of Yankton and pushed for the creation of the Dakota Territory. With Todd's help, Yankton became the first capital of Dakota, and Todd served as the territory's first member of the U.S. House of Representatives.

 Want to know more? See www.usd.edu/nplhist/02Todd.pdf

A homestead near Sioux Falls, mid-1880s

PIONEER POET

Kate Campbell was part of an African American family who settled in the Yankton area in the 1880s. Campbell was often sick, so she did not attend school until she was 12, but she loved learning, reading, and especially writing. Her first poem was published in the *Christian Recorder*, a popular church paper. Later, another poem was published in the *Indianapolis Freeman*, a widely read African American national weekly. Campbell denounced bigotry and called on African Americans to "stand firmly as a race" until "the darkest night gives way to the brightest day." She continued to write poems that were widely published.

By 1861, South Dakotans convinced the U.S. Congress to create the Dakota Territory. This was the first step toward becoming a state. The original Dakota Territory included what is now North Dakota and South Dakota, Montana, and part of Wyoming. Yankton was named the capital. Two years later, Montana and Wyoming split off from the Dakota Territory.

During this time, about 1,000 whites and a handful of African Americans lived in South Dakota. At first, only white residents of the territory were allowed to vote. Over the next several decades, the territory's population exploded, as settlers of various backgrounds came to the prairies and plains. By 1880, 400 African American pioneers lived in South Dakota. They wanted to vote as much as other settlers, and they demanded their rights.

Soon South Dakotans of all backgrounds were pushing for more of a voice. They wanted statehood.

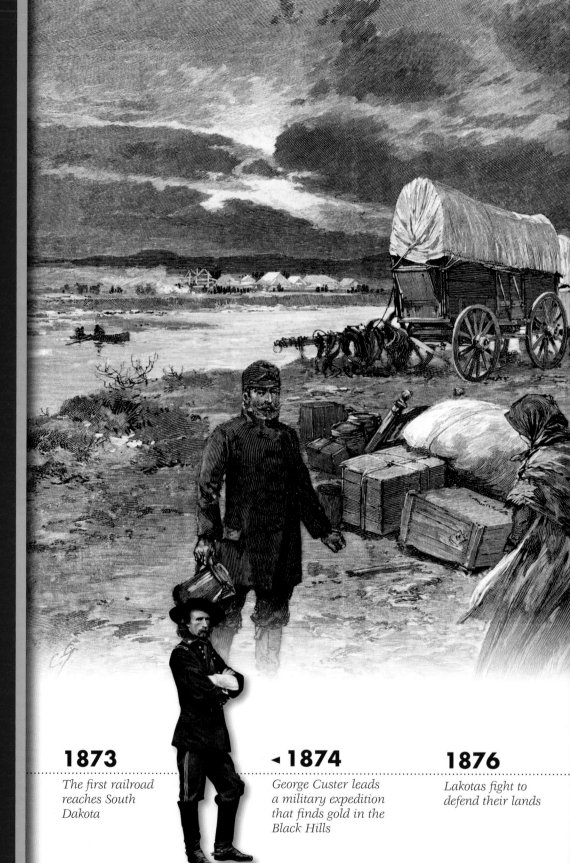

44

READ ABOUT

Settlers claiming
land in what
is now South
Dakota, 1890

1873

The first railroad
reaches South
Dakota

◄ 1874

George Custer leads
a military expedition
that finds gold in the
Black Hills

1876

Lakotas fight to
defend their lands

C H A P T E R   F O U R

GROWTH AND CHANGE

★

SOUTH DAKOTA HAD WIDE-OPEN SPACES, AND THE BLACK HILLS WERE FILLED WITH PRECIOUS NATURAL RESOURCES. Americans from the East and immigrants from around the world were all eager to call South Dakota home. They brought their old ideas with them as they created new towns in South Dakota.

1878–1887

Thousands of homesteaders claim land during the Dakota land boom

1889 ►

South Dakota becomes the 40th state

1890

U.S. troops kill about 350 Lakotas at the Wounded Knee Massacre

The crew of a Union vessel, the USS *Hunchback*, on the James River, 1864

During the 1870s, huge swarms of grasshoppers sometimes destroyed crops across South Dakota. In 1874, almost all the corn grown between Yankton and Sioux Falls was lost.

IMMIGRANTS ARRIVE

Most of the first white settlers in South Dakota came from New England, New York, and other parts of the Northeast. Most traced their family roots to Great Britain. These newcomers, called Yankees, believed in working hard and building strong communities.

The growth of new towns went slowly. In 1862, Dakota Sioux in western Minnesota battled newcomers, and South Dakota settlers feared they would also have to fight for the land. Some fled to Yankton, and others simply left the territory. The fear of Indian attack lasted for several years, keeping new families from entering the region. The Civil War, which began in 1861, also hindered settlement. Several million men fought in the war between Northern and Southern states, and many others got jobs making war supplies in the East, so few people moved westward during this period.

After the Civil War ended in 1865, European immigrants began joining Yankees in the Dakota Territory.

Norwegians were the first major group. In the decades to come, they were joined by Swedes and Danes. Czechs, Germans, and Russian Germans followed. Many of the new arrivals worked as farmers, raising wheat, corn, and other crops in the prairies east of the Missouri River. Fur trapping and trading were no longer profitable in South Dakota, because most of the beavers had been killed and there was little demand for other furs.

Q8 WHO WERE THE RUSSIAN GERMANS?

A8 During the 18th century, large groups of Germans settled in Russia, where they continued to keep their own language and their own culture. Beginning in the 1870s, thousands of these Russian Germans migrated to the United States to escape unfair treatment and service in the Russian army. In South Dakota, many settled in Eureka.

IRON AND GOLD

Steamboats remained a major source of transportation in the Dakotas until 1873. That year, the first "iron horse," or train, reached the territory. Railways ran to Yankton and Vermillion, making it easier to transport people and goods. Over the decades, the railroad lines

WOW

Sally Campbell, an African American cook, traveled with George Custer's Seventh Cavalry in 1874. She was the first non-Indian woman to visit the Black Hills. She later settled in Galena, in western South Dakota.

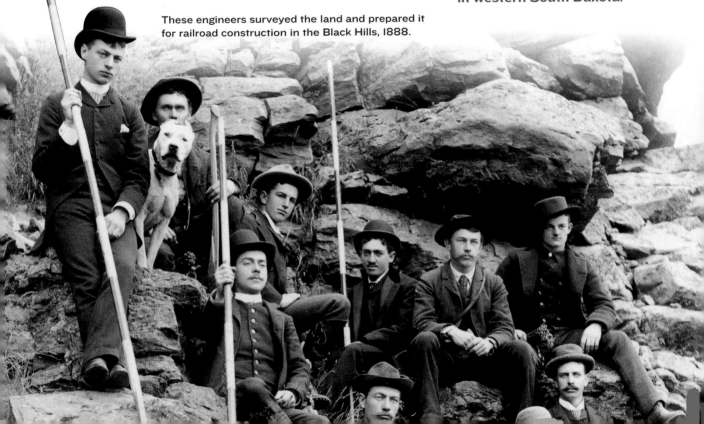

These engineers surveyed the land and prepared it for railroad construction in the Black Hills, 1888.

MINI-BIO

SITTING BULL: DEFENDER OF NATIVE LANDS

Tatanka-Iyotanka (c. 1831–1890), a Hunkpapa Lakota leader and medicine man, is generally known by his English name, Sitting Bull. In the 1860s, Sitting Bull battled U.S. troops in the Dakotas several times. When miners rushed to the Black Hills to search for gold, Sitting Bull swore he and his forces would keep the Americans out. After the Battle of the Little Bighorn, U.S. troops chased Sitting Bull and other Lakotas across South Dakota. For a time, Sitting Bull lived in Canada to avoid going to a reservation. Finally, in 1881, his people were starving because so few bison remained, and he agreed to move to a South Dakota reservation. Sitting Bull's courage and leadership continue to inspire people to this day.

Want to know more? See www.pbs.org/weta/thewest/people/s_z/sittingbull.htm

WOW

African American U.S. Army regiments known as the Buffalo Soldiers helped keep the peace in the 1860s and 1870s. They were often given poor equipment, shoddy rifles, and old horses. But a dozen Buffalo Soldiers earned Congressional Medals of Honor defending western communities.

slowly moved westward across the territory. Towns along the lines tended to grow, and those far away from them died. In some cases, entire towns moved to be closer to the railroads.

The railroads helped bring new settlers to the state. So did the lure of gold. As early as the 1850s, U.S. soldiers exploring the Black Hills reported seeing gold. The discovery of gold in Montana in the 1860s stimulated interest in the Black Hills. In 1874, Lieutenant Colonel George Custer led an expedition into the Black Hills to search for gold. When Custer and his men found gold, word spread across the nation. A gold rush began the next year, and miners poured into the region.

The arrival of the miners threatened the Lakota Sioux who lived in and around the Black Hills. During the 1850s, Lakota leader Sitting Bull had warned U.S. soldiers not to build forts or roads in the area.

Under an 1868 treaty, the U.S. government recognized the Lakotas' ancestral lands in western South Dakota as a reservation. Lakotas did not want limits placed on where they could live or hunt on their land. The 1868 treaty said settlers could not go to the Black Hills, but white miners ignored it.

The town of Deadwood during the Black Hills gold rush, 1870s

In 1876, Sitting Bull, a Lakota medicine man named Crazy Horse, and others led Lakotas and their allies in a war against the United States. At the Battle of the Little Bighorn in Montana, Indians killed Custer and about 200 of his men. Soon, however, U.S. troops rounded up Native Americans on the northern plains, and the Black Hills were opened for white mining and settlement.

Deadwood and Lead (pronounced "leed") became the major towns in the Black Hills. They attracted miners, cowhands, and merchants who sold supplies. The miners were people from many backgrounds, including African Americans and Chinese. Deadwood

The Homestake Gold Mine in the Black Hills was the largest deposit of gold ever found in North America. It continued to produce gold until 2002.

MINI-BIO

FEE LEE WONG: SUCCESSFUL MERCHANT

Around 1870, Fee Lee Wong (1846–1921) left his homeland in China for the United States. Wong worked as a cook in the Black Hills. When robbers attacked the miners, Wong stood with them and helped fight. The miners rewarded his bravery by granting him the rights to two mines. Wong sold one and used the money to open a store in Deadwood's Chinatown, where most Chinese immigrants lived. In time, he bought several buildings and became one of the town's most successful merchants. His main building in Deadwood, called the Wing Tsue, survived until 2005. Archaeologists plan to study the site to look for items once used by Chinese Americans in Deadwood.

? Want to know more? See www.deadwoodmagazine.com/back_issues/article.php?read_id=113

became one of the wildest towns in the West. It was filled with saloons where people gambled and sometimes got into gunfights. "Wild Bill" Hickok, a sheriff and gunman, was killed in a Deadwood bar. Martha Jane Cannary, a frontier scout, was better known as Calamity Jane. She and Hickok are buried next to each other in Deadwood.

The gold rush ended in the 1880s, but people continued to work in the Black Hills. Some people still mined gold, while others cut trees for timber or raised cattle, horses, and other livestock.

THE DAKOTA BOOM

In 1862, Congress had passed the Homestead Act. This law let people have 160 acres (65 ha) of public land for free if they lived on it for five years and improved it in some way. Farming was the most common form of improvement. Settlers could claim the land in just six months if they paid for it. The people who settled on the land were called homesteaders.

From 1878 to 1887, thousands came to South Dakota to claim land. Investors also claimed some of the land, hoping to sell it for a profit in the future. During that time, people filed claims for more than 24 million acres (9.7 million ha) of land. The home-

When families traveled west, they often packed all their belongings in covered wagons for the journey.

steaders included Benjamin, Patrick, and Mary Blair, whose parents had once been enslaved. They started a community of African Americans in Sully County called the Blair Colony.

Families traveled by wagon or railroad to the land they claimed. They used heavy-duty plows to churn up the prairie and prepare it for planting. Families had to dig deep wells for water. For heat, they sometimes burned buffalo chips (dried manure) if they could not find wood. To heat pans for cooking, settlers twisted together clumps of prairie grass and burned it. Children

A sod house in Newell

Picture Yourself...

Living in a Sod House

You just moved to the South Dakota prairie from the East. Finally, your family has its own land to farm. The first thing you need to do when you arrive in South Dakota is build a house, but there are few trees around. Instead, you and your parents build a **sod** house. You dig up thick slices of the prairie—the tangle of prairie grass roots holds the soil together—and cut it into bricks. You stack the bricks to create a small house. Inside the house is a hard dirt floor. Dirt occasionally falls from the sod roof, and water sometimes streams in when it rains. Your sod house is cramped, so you don't spend much time inside it. But on the bright side, it is cool in the summer and warm in the winter. It won't catch fire, like a wooden house might. And you can grow flowers on your roof!

WORD TO KNOW

sod *soil thickly packed together with grass and roots*

helped on the family farm, and some attended school in a private home. As towns grew, schools were built.

Over time, agriculture became more mechanized. Farmers began using steam-powered machines that could pull plows or cut crops. The machines were expensive, and most farmers still relied on animal power for their work. But mechanized farming slowly spread across South Dakota.

PATH TO STATEHOOD

In 1880, just under 100,000 people lived in South Dakota. That number would almost triple in only 10 years. The region's largest towns were east of the Missouri River, but ranching and mining also drew settlers west of the river. Dakotans began pushing for dividing the Dakota

South Dakota: From Territory to Statehood

(1861–1889)

This map shows the original South Dakota territory and the area (in yellow) that became the state of South Dakota.

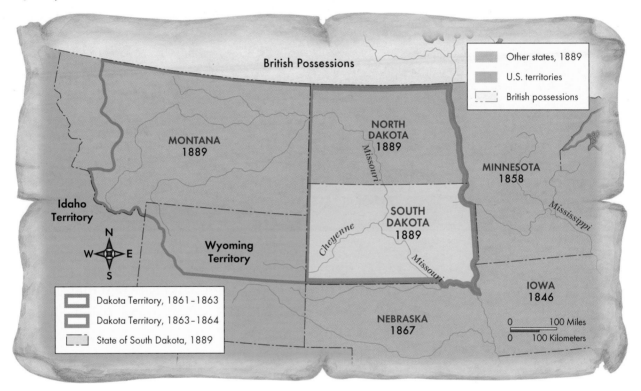

	Other states, 1889
	U.S. territories
	British possessions

British Possessions

MONTANA
1889

NORTH
DAKOTA
1889

MINNESOTA
1858

Idaho
Territory

Missouri

SOUTH
DAKOTA
1889

Mississippi

Wyoming
Territory

Cheyenne

Missouri

IOWA
1846

N
W E
S

NEBRASKA
1867

0 — 100 Miles
0 — 100 Kilometers

	Dakota Territory, 1861–1863
	Dakota Territory, 1863–1864
	State of South Dakota, 1889

Territory into two states, and Congress agreed in 1889. South Dakota became the 40th state. Its new capital was Pierre, a town across from Fort Pierre on the east side of the Missouri River.

WOUNDED KNEE

Soon after the celebrations for statehood ended, violence erupted in South Dakota. In 1890, a new religion reached Indians in South Dakota. Followers of the Ghost

WOW

South Dakota entered the Union as a "dry" state, meaning buying and selling alcohol was illegal. That law stood until 1896.

A scene from the Wounded Knee Massacre, 1890

Dance religion believed that special dances and prayers would help Native American nations regain their lands and way of life. The U.S. government believed the spread of the Ghost Dance was dangerous.

The government feared that Sitting Bull, the great Lakota leader, would practice the religion. If he did, other Sioux might also accept it. Lakota police hired by the U.S. government came to the Standing Rock Reservation to arrest Sitting Bull, but instead they killed him. The Ghost Dancers fled, and some ended up near Wounded Knee Creek on the Pine Ridge Reservation in southwestern South Dakota. U.S. troops tracked them there. On December 29, 1890, someone fired a gun, perhaps accidentally, and the troops opened fire on the camp of Indian families. About 350 Lakotas died at the Wounded Knee Massacre. The Ghost Dance religion died as well.

POLITICAL CHANGES

By the 1890s, railroads were spreading across South Dakota. Farmers in the state began to fear that growth, because companies that owned the railroads controlled the economy. Farmers thought that these companies charged too much to carry grain to mills. South Dakota farmers struggled with bad weather, but banks expected them to pay back loans whether they could afford to or not. Some farming families formed the Populist Party to fight for their interests. In the late 1890s, Populists dominated the state government. They changed the state **constitution** so voters could propose

WORD TO KNOW

constitution *a written document that contains all the governing principles of a state or country*

SEE IT HERE!

THE CORN PALACE

In 1892, South Dakotans held the Corn Belt Exposition in Mitchell to honor farmers and their crops and to show how fertile their soil was. Corn and other crops decorated the outside of the building. From that came the Corn Palace—an assembly hall and theater covered with corn. Each year, volunteers create images of South Dakota life using only colored corn and grains—more than 40 tons of them! Inside the hall are more murals made of corn. The current Corn Palace—the third—opened in 1921. Its top is covered with onion-shaped domes, and visitors come to admire the "corny" art, which represents agricultural history in the state.

The Corn Palace in Mitchell

MINI-BIO

MAMIE SHIELDS PYLE: FIGHTER FOR WOMEN'S RIGHTS

Born in New Jersey, Mamie Shields Pyle (1866–1949) settled in Huron, South Dakota, in 1889. Pyle took a strong interest in politics and demanded suffrage, or the right to vote, for women. During the 1910s, she was president of the South Dakota State Suffrage Association. With her leadership, South Dakota women won the right to vote in 1918—two years before all U.S. women won that right. Toward the end of her life, Pyle was named the state's Mother of the Year. This honor came after she proudly saw her daughter Gladys become South Dakota's first female lawmaker.

❓ **Want to know more?** See www.sd4history.com/Unit7/notableSDlesson2.htm

Governor Peter Norbeck of the Progressive Party was in office from 1917 to 1921.

Q8 WHAT WAS PROGRESSIVISM?

A8 Progressivism was a movement to improve lives for workers, farmers, women, and children. Progressives wanted to give the average American more control in politics and end the influence of big business.

laws, a process called the initiative. Voters could also reject or accept certain laws passed by the legislature, a process called the referendum.

The Populists were not able to stop the overwhelming power of huge corporations in South Dakota's politics and economy. But their efforts led to many reforms and paved the way for a new effort led by the Progressives. A Progressive named Peter Norbeck served as governor from 1917 to 1921. Under Norbeck, the state government offered low-interest loans to farmers. It also provided insurance for crops damaged by hail and paid money to workers injured on the job. The Progressive movement remained strong in South Dakota for several decades.

WORLD WAR I AND AFTER

In 1914, fighting broke out among several European nations, marking the start of World War I. The United States entered the war in 1917, and South Dakotans did their part to help. About 32,000 of them joined the military. Farmers increased production, because the U.S. government was sending food to its allies. The demand for crops led to more money for farmers.

When the war ended in 1918, farmers were still enjoying high prices for their crops. But nature and world events would conspire to create many challenges in the coming decades.

A South Dakota farmer plows a beet field, early 1900s

A view of
Aberdeen,
early 1900s

1930–1936

*Severe drought strikes
South Dakota*

1933

*New Deal programs
begin helping South
Dakotans during the
Great Depression*

▲1941–1945

*Thousands of South
Dakotans, including Sioux
code talkers, fight in World
War II*

CHAPTER FIVE

MORE MODERN TIMES

★

FOR MOST OF THE NATION, THE EARLY 1920s WERE A PROSPEROUS TIME. But that was not the case for South Dakota farmers. The demand for their crops fell, so prices fell. Some farmers lost their land because they couldn't pay their debts, and banks began to close. Still, some South Dakotans bought radios and cars. And the government built more paved roads, which attracted tourists to the state.

1946
Work begins on four dams across the Missouri River

1979
Lakotas are awarded more than $100 million for the loss of their lands in the Black Hills but refuse to take it

▲21st century
South Dakota is home to banks and credit card companies

Mount Rushmore was under construction from 1927 to 1941.

SEE IT HERE!

MOUNT RUSHMORE

In 1923, South Dakota historian Doane Robinson promoted the idea of carving a giant sculpture into the rocks of the Black Hills to attract more tourists to the area. U.S. senator Peter Norbeck pressed for federal support. Robinson contacted artist Gutzon Borglum, who chose Mount Rushmore as the site. From 1927 to 1941, workers cut giant heads of four American presidents—George Washington, Thomas Jefferson, Theodore Roosevelt, and Abraham Lincoln—into the side of the mountain. Today, more than 2.5 million people visit Mount Rushmore each year, making it South Dakota's most popular tourist attraction.

HARD TIMES

South Dakota's farm problems worsened after 1929, when the entire country entered the Great Depression, the worst economic crisis in U.S. history. Across the country, millions of people lost their jobs and sometimes their homes. Thousands of banks closed, wiping out people's savings. Many South Dakota farmers lost their land. Those who continued to farm faced severe

The first speed limit in Sioux Falls was enacted in 1903. Cars could not go faster than 7 miles per hour (11 kph) on straight roads and 4 mph (6 kph) around corners.

drought in the 1930s and watched as the fertile topsoil blew away in "black blizzards."

In 1933, President Franklin D. Roosevelt began a series of programs called the New Deal, which were intended to relieve suffering from lack of work and income during the Great Depression. Some New Deal programs put people to work building libraries or improving parks. Others helped farmers. Under one program, farmers in South Dakota and elsewhere received money if they did not grow certain crops. Reducing the supply caused prices to rise. The government money helped farmers pay their debts, and they could receive government loans at low interest rates. Farmers also received money if they grew crops such as soybeans, which were good for the soil.

BLACK BLIZZARDS

One of the worst droughts in South Dakota history began in 1930. By 1933, strong winds sometimes picked up the dry soil and carried it for miles. The clouds of dirt blackened the skies in what were called black blizzards. The blowing dirt buried cars and tractors. One newspaper reported, "The roofs of sheds stuck out through drifts deeper than a man is tall." Rainfall finally returned to normal in 1936, ending the drought.

These laborers for the Works Progress Administration, a New Deal program, help build a bridge near Pierre.

MEDICAL PIONEER

The daughter of a doctor, Abbie Jarvis (1854–1931) waited a long time before pursuing her own medical career. She and her husband moved to South Dakota in 1880, eventually settling in Faulkton. When she was in her late 30s, Jarvis went to medical school. She graduated in 1898, becoming South Dakota's first female doctor. She made house calls to remote farms, often delivering babies. She safely brought more than 600 children into the world, and they were sometimes called Jarvis babies. She continued her medical practice through the 1920s, almost until the time of her death.

WORLD WAR II

The New Deal programs helped millions of Americans, but they did not end the Great Depression. Only the coming of World War II ended the economic problems. War broke out in Europe in September 1939, as Great Britain, France, and other countries battled German forces. U.S. factories were soon bustling with activity, as the country supplied its European allies. Then on December 7, 1941, Japan launched a surprise attack on the U.S. naval base in Pearl Harbor, Hawai'i. The United States declared war on Japan, Germany, and Italy.

Troops of the 34th Infantry—including soldiers from Minnesota, North Dakota, and South Dakota—in Italy, 1943

MINI-BIO

JOE FOSS: WAR HERO AND MORE

Joe Foss (1915–2003) was just 11 when he went to an air show in Sioux Falls. After that, he knew he wanted to fly. He already had his pilot's license when World War II began, and soon he was flying fighter planes for the U.S. Marines. Foss became a national hero after shooting down 26 planes and winning the Congressional Medal of Honor. After the war, he entered politics, eventually serving as South Dakota's governor for four years. In 1959, he became president of the American Football League, which later became part of the National Football League.

? **Want to know more?** See www.arlingtoncemetery.net/jjfoss.htm

Native American code talkers assigned to a marine unit during World War II

Once again, thousands of South Dakotans volunteered to fight. Many Sioux soldiers won praise for their battlefield skills, while others worked as "code talkers," sending and receiving messages in codes spoken in their native languages. These codes were virtually impossible to break since almost no one except Native Americans could speak the languages on which they were based. Eleven Sioux from South Dakota served as code talkers during the war.

Many South Dakotans moved to other states to take jobs in factories making military equipment. The farmers who remained in South Dakota stepped up their crop production to feed soldiers fighting around the world. Their flax was turned into linen, which was used to make uniforms. And South Dakota soybeans were turned into oil used in cooking.

Thousands of Americans came to South Dakota to train or work at military bases. The Sioux Falls airport was taken over by the Army Air Corps and served as a training base for radio operators. Both Pierre and Rapid City also had army air bases. And in the Black Hills, near Edgemont, the government stored ammunition.

POSTWAR CHANGES

After the war ended in 1945, many South Dakotans continued to work at or near military bases. But the daily activities of most people in the state revolved around farming. They either raised crops and livestock, transported them, or provided services and equipment to farmers. Still, life was changing in South Dakota. Electricity, which had once been limited to towns, was

The busy streets of Aberdeen, 1960s

reaching more farms, and car ownership continued to grow. The state had lost population in the 1930s, but the numbers were inching back up. Just over 650,000 people lived there in 1950, about 10,000 more than in 1940.

Most of the growth occurred in larger towns and cities. In rural areas, young people left farms to find jobs in towns and cities. The drain of rural residents continued when new interstate highways appeared in the early 1960s. One cut the state in half from east to west. The other traveled from north to south in the eastern part of the state. Towns far from the highway began to die—just as others had when the railroad tracks bypassed them in the 1880s.

Between 1946 and 1966, one of the biggest projects in the state was the construction of four dams across the Missouri River. The dams created huge **reservoirs**, which covered about 500,000 acres (202,000 ha) of land, including some valuable farmland. The dams were built to help control floods and provide **irrigation** for farmland. They also created electricity, and the new lakes became popular recreation areas.

LAKOTA STRUGGLES

Through the 20th century, Sioux families often had trouble adjusting to life on reservations. Lakotas in particular struggled to become farmers and ranchers as the government wanted. Some rented their land to white farmers, while other Sioux left the reservations to find jobs out of state.

In 1934, the U.S. Commissioner of Indian Affairs issued an order that gave all Native Americans greater freedom to follow their traditional culture. Congress passed a law to allow them more freedom to run their own affairs. Still, for the Sioux of South Dakota, life remained difficult.

WORDS TO KNOW

reservoirs *artificial lakes or tanks for storing water*

irrigation *watering land by artificial means to promote plant growth*

In 1979, a U.S. court said the Lakota people should receive more than $100 million to pay for their earlier loss of the Black Hills. Lakotas refused the money, because they still wanted the land.

RUSSELL MEANS: LAKOTA ACTIVIST

Russell Means (1939–) was born to a Yankton mother and an Oglala father on the Pine Ridge Indian Reservation. In 1969, he joined the American Indian Movement (AIM). Means wanted the U.S. government to return Indian lands and treat Native Americans fairly. He joined protests at Mount Rushmore and Plymouth Rock before going to Wounded Knee in 1973. Though he is no longer with AIM, he continues to speak out for Indian rights. He also encourages Indians to explore their cultures.

? Want to know more? See www.russellmeans.com

By the late 1960s, some Sioux wanted to take action. Russell Means, an Oglala Lakota, became one of the leaders of the American Indian Movement (AIM). AIM wanted the U.S. government to help end poverty and legal inequality for all Indians. In 1973, Means and other Sioux went to Wounded Knee to protest conditions on the reservations. A gun battle broke out between some of the Indians and U.S. officials, and

Russell Means, Dennis Banks, and Carter Camp (left to right) make a peace agreement with Methodist bishop James Armstrong at Wounded Knee, 1970s.

Grain being harvested on a South Dakota farm

two Indians died. Once again, Wounded Knee was associated with violence. But the efforts of AIM led the government to give Native Americans more self-rule and protection for their traditional ways.

RECENT TIMES

During the late 1970s and early 1980s, South Dakota farmers faced new economic problems. Farmers were too successful: they grew so much grain that prices fell. But as in the 1930s, the farmers still had debts to pay, with no money to pay them. Over time, more small farmers went out of business, while others turned to part-time work to pay their bills. Farmers with more land were usually able to survive and often grew by taking over other farms.

New industries came to South Dakota in the 1980s. Changes in state banking laws attracted several large banks to Sioux Falls. They ran their credit card services in the city, where the population grew by 23 percent in

A ranger takes a group on a hike through Badlands National Park.

the 1990s. Sioux Falls also became the center for health care in the state. The arrival of new companies drew new immigrants to South Dakota. Most came from Asia or Latin America. Tourism also thrived.

In the 21st century, the farm economy once again boomed in South Dakota. The United States began looking for new sources of energy, so it would not have to rely on oil. Fuel could be made from corn, soybeans, and other crops, and South Dakota farmers saw prices for these goods rise as demand increased.

New Energy Sources

The demand for new sources of energy could bring major changes to South Dakota. In 2007, a Texas company considered South Dakota for the site of a new oil refinery. The plant would process oil mined in Alberta, Canada. Not all South Dakotans thought the plant was a good idea.

PRO

The Elk Point City Council welcomed the new refinery. The plant, town leaders said, would "enhance America's energy independence." America would have to buy less oil from foreign countries that don't always agree with U.S. policies. The refinery would also create thousands of new jobs, as workers would be needed to build the plant and run it.

CON

Residents who opposed the refinery feared the pollution it might bring. University of South Dakota professor Dean Spader wondered, "How many types of [pollution] exist? How much of each will [the refinery] produce? And how much will be emitted into the air and water?" Others said the demand for workers at the refinery would raise salaries in the area, and smaller local companies wouldn't be able to afford to pay them. The small businesses would lose workers to the new refinery.

South Dakota has great natural beauty, low taxes that make it attractive to businesses, and a hardworking labor force. Many South Dakotans believe this combination makes the state well-prepared to face the challenges of the future.

70

READ ABOUT

Visitors at Mount Rushmore

CHAPTER SIX

PEOPLE

★

MANY OF THE TOWNS ON SOUTH DAKOTA'S PRAIRIES AND PLAINS ARE GROWING. The population rise is fueled by new arrivals from Spanish-speaking countries, as well as Africa and Asia. But some parts of the state are still sparsely populated. Take a drive and you might see just one or two homes for miles and miles. South Dakota is still a land of wide-open spaces.

South Dakota Population Growth

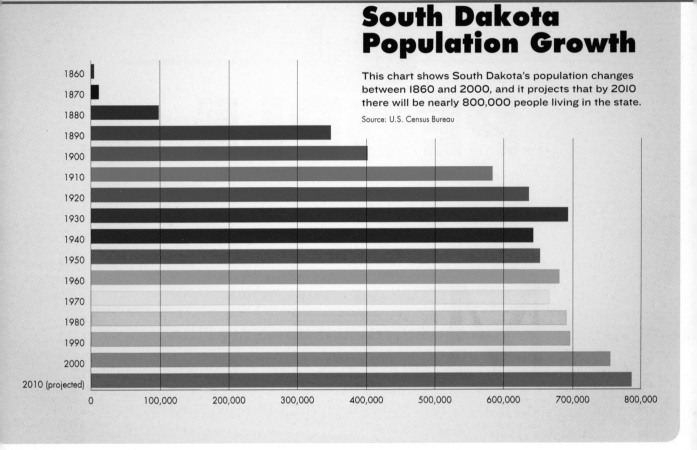

This chart shows South Dakota's population changes between 1860 and 2000, and it projects that by 2010 there will be nearly 800,000 people living in the state.

Source: U.S. Census Bureau

AT HOME IN SOUTH DAKOTA

Fewer than 800,000 people live in South Dakota's 77,117 square miles (199,732 sq km). That gives the state one of the lowest population densities in the country, with just over 11 people for every square mile (4 per sq km). The largest population centers are found at either end of the state near the two major cities, Sioux Falls and Rapid City.

ONE STATE, DIFFERENT BACKGROUNDS

Since the coming of American settlers in the 19th century, South Dakotans have generally traced their roots to either Sioux tribes or European nations. Today, Native

Big City Life

This list shows the population of South Dakota's biggest cities.

Sioux Falls	139,517
Rapid City	62,167
Aberdeen	24,098
Watertown	20,265
Brookings	18,715

Source: U.S. Census Bureau

Americans make up about 9 percent of the population, one of the highest percentages among the states.

The state's white population includes people from the British Isles, **Scandinavia**, and Germany. In 2000, about 40 percent of South Dakotans said they had family ties to Germany, making German Americans the largest ethnic group. They were followed by Norwegians with 15 percent and Irish with 10 percent.

In recent years, the Hispanic population of South Dakota has seen marked growth. From 1990 to 2005, the number of Hispanics grew from about 5,000 to more than 14,000. Most of the new arrivals came from Mexico and Central America. Many took jobs working in meat-processing plants in the southeastern part of the state. The number of South Dakotans of Asian descent is also small but growing, and most settle in the more urban areas of the eastern part of the state. In the past, few African Americans settled in the state, and while their numbers

The Oglala Lakota, with more than 42,000 members, is the largest tribe in South Dakota.

WORD TO KNOW

Scandinavia *a region of northern Europe made up of Sweden, Norway, Denmark, Finland, and Iceland*

A couple captures the view at Badlands National Park.

Q8 WHO ARE THE HUTTERITES?

A8 The Hutterites are a small Protestant group who trace their roots to Russian German settlers of South Dakota. The Hutterites own all their property as a group and live in communities called colonies. They oppose war and live simple lives, often making their own clothing and furniture. South Dakota's Hutterites are excellent farmers, raising most of the turkeys and hogs produced in the state.

WORD TO KNOW

refugees *people who flee their homelands because of war or natural disasters*

People QuickFacts

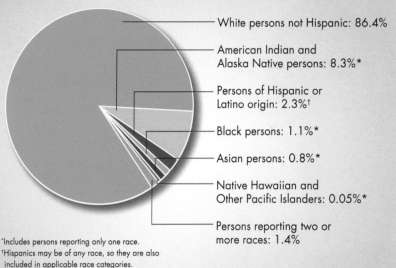

White persons not Hispanic: 86.4%

American Indian and Alaska Native persons: 8.3%*

Persons of Hispanic or Latino origin: 2.3%†

Black persons: 1.1%*

Asian persons: 0.8%*

Native Hawaiian and Other Pacific Islanders: 0.05%*

Persons reporting two or more races: 1.4%

*Includes persons reporting only one race.
†Hispanics may be of any race, so they are also included in applicable race categories.
Source: U.S. Census Bureau, 2007 estimate

are slowly growing today, they remain a tiny part of the population. Some African newcomers are **refugees**. In 2007, 40 refugees from Burundi settled in Sioux Falls.

CITY LIFE, RURAL LIFE

Once, most South Dakotans lived a rural life in small towns. Since 1990, the state's population has become slightly more urban than rural. And modern technology such as satellites and the Internet connect remote parts of South Dakota to the larger world.

Sioux Falls is the major urban center in the state. Suburbs are growing around the city as businesses and workers move to the area.

Most of South Dakota is still a land of small towns. The state has strong, closely knit communities, where people help each other during bad times and come together to celebrate the good. Still, many young South Dakotans think their small hometowns don't provide enough entertainment or good jobs. They often leave the towns for larger cities both in and out of South Dakota. In 2000, 31 counties in the state reported shrinking populations. Most of them were in the central part of the state, far from cities.

Where South Dakotans Live

The colors on this map indicate population density throughout the state. The darker the color, the more people live there.

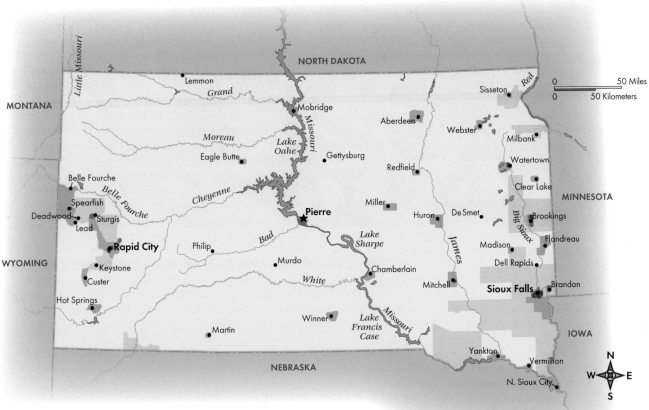

People per square mile

	1,000 or more
	250 to 1,000
	50 to 250
	10 to 50
	10 or fewer

RESERVATION LIFE

South Dakota's nine Indian reservations are home to just over 100,000 people. On the reservations, many Sioux blend their traditional spiritual beliefs with modern ways of life. They might go to a sweat lodge, a hut heated with hot stones. By sitting in a sweat lodge, Sioux ritually purify themselves. They then might go home and watch satellite TV. Native Americans on reservations face higher rates of poverty than other people, but the Sioux have made progress in starting businesses that provide jobs for many of their people.

A farmers' market in Sioux Falls

HOW TO TALK LIKE A SOUTH DAKOTAN

When you go to a grocery store, your purchases will likely be put in a "sack" rather than a "bag." And when you visit the state capital, talk like a native and call it "Peer"—South Dakotans don't use the French pronunciation of Pierre (pee-AIR). Say "East River" and "West River" to describe the eastern and western halves of the state, and folks might think you're a local. And if you meet some Dakota Sioux, you can greet them in their native language by saying *Hau koda*, or "Welcome, friend!"

HOW TO EAT LIKE A SOUTH DAKOTAN

You'd expect a farm state to produce lots of hearty meals, and South Dakota doesn't let you down. Beef is often on the menu, but so are wild animals from the state's forests and fish from the state's streams. Grains such as wheat and corn are used in many dishes. And the different settlers of the state, from Sioux to Germans, have added their favorite foods to the state's meals.

MENU

WHAT'S ON THE MENU IN SOUTH DAKOTA?

★ ★ ★

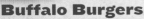

Buffalo burger

Buffalo Burgers

Bison (buffalo) were once almost extinct. Now South Dakota ranchers raise the shaggy beasts for their meat. Bison is low in fat compared to beef. Besides burgers, bison meat is also used for steaks and sausages.

Wasna/Pemmican

When bison and other game were scarce on the plains, the Sioux turned to a food that could last for years. They called it *wasna* (wah-SHNA), though today it's better known as pemmican. Wasna is packed with protein and other things your body needs. Traditional wasna was made with dried bison meat, chokecherries (a type of fruit), and animal fat.

Pheasant

Hunters stalk these game birds over two-thirds of the state, and they've come up with lots of ways to prepare them. Pheasant meat is used in soups and casseroles, while some folks prefer it simply roasted.

Indian Fry Bread

This typical Plains Indian dish is made by frying bread dough in oil. Some people cover it with toppings to make an "Indian taco," while others eat it with sugar or berries.

TRY THIS RECIPE
Kuchen

Kuchen

The Russian Germans of South Dakota perfected this sweet treat, which is the German word for "cake." People make many different types of kuchen, which can look like a coffee cake or a pie. Most recipes include a custard filling, and some kuchen are filled with fruit. Have an adult nearby to help you make this apple kuchen.

Batter Ingredients:
1 cup milk
2 eggs
⅔ cup flour
2 teaspoons sugar
½ teaspoon grated lemon zest
½ teaspoon salt
2 tablespoons butter

Filling Ingredients:
2 cups thickly sliced apples
2 tablespoons butter
3 tablespoons sugar
½ teaspoon cinnamon

Instructions:
1. Preheat the oven to 400°F.
2. Mix the milk, eggs, flour, sugar, salt, and lemon zest together in a bowl to make the batter.
3. Melt the butter in a skillet. Put the melted butter in a 9-inch pie plate and then pour the batter into the pie plate.
4. Bake the kuchen for 30 to 35 minutes, until it is golden brown.
5. While the kuchen is baking, peel and slice the apples.
6. Melt the butter in a skillet, and then cook the apples, sugar, and cinnamon in the butter over medium heat until the apples are tender.
7. After removing the kuchen from the oven, pour the apple filling in its center, and serve immediately.

Some South Dakota public schools hold classes just four days per week. Cutting out a day helps towns save money. The students make up the time by having longer hours on each of the four days.

EDUCATION

On school days, South Dakota's students in grades K–12 head out to either public or private schools. The state has just over 800 schools, including many on reservations. At Indian schools, students learn their native language along with the same subjects taught in other schools.

The state's largest public university is South Dakota State University in Brookings, which has strong programs in agriculture and nursing. The University of South Dakota in Vermillion is home to the state's only medical school and law school.

A WAY WITH WORDS

Many South Dakotans have written novels that delve into their experiences with the state's lonely prairies and rugged mountains. Hamlin Garland didn't spend much time in South Dakota, but his book *Main-Travelled Roads* described pioneer life in the state. O. E. Rolvaag, a Norwegian immigrant, worked and studied in South Dakota and wrote three novels that illustrate the pioneer experience. During World War II, Borghild Dahl wrote books about her own blindness and immigrant life.

More recently, Lakota writer Virginia Driving Hawk Sneve has entertained and educated both children and adults with her work. Her children's books include *When Thunders Spoke* and *Jimmy Yellow Hawk*. Paul Goble, who lives in Rapid

MINI-BIO

LAURA INGALLS WILDER: PIONEER WRITER

Laura Ingalls Wilder (1867–1957) spent part of her childhood in a house near De Smet, South Dakota. She watched the prairie change and towns grow, and later wrote a series of nine children's books about her pioneer childhood, known as the Little House series. Her books have sold tens of millions of copies around the world and sparked the hit TV show *Little House on the Prairie*. By telling her family's stories, Wilder also told the history of South Dakota pioneer life.

? Want to know more? See www. lauraingallswilderhome.com

City, has also written and illustrated many children's books that often deal with Native American life.

VISUAL ARTS

Visual art has a long history in South Dakota. Thousands of years ago, Native people carved images into rocks, often showing human or animal figures. Several hundred years ago, Sioux artists recorded their people's history by drawing images on dried animal skins. Many modern Sioux artists were influenced by Oscar Howe, a Yanktonai Nakota who blended traditional Native American forms with the ideas of modern art. Other artists in South Dakota include Terry Redlin, who was inspired by South Dakota communities and wildlife, and Harvey Dunn, who illustrated scenes of American life for many magazines.

Artist Terry Redlin

MINI-BIO

OSCAR HOWE: PAINTER

Oscar Howe (1915–1983) was the great-grandson of two Yanktonai Nakota chiefs. Growing up on the Crow Creek Reservation, he learned about Sioux history and culture. He wanted to draw the stories he heard, but his father did not want him to become an artist and took away his pencils. Oscar then found some charcoal and used that to draw. As an adult, Howe blended traditional Indian techniques with the skills he learned in art school. His paintings often featured geometric shapes, such as triangles, lines, and arcs. He continues to influence South Dakota artists today.

? Want to know more? See www.dakotadiscovery.com/subcategory.cfm?cat_id=8&subcat_Id=20

MINI-BIO

OSCAR MICHEAUX: HOMESTEADER AND FILMMAKER

In 1904, near the Rosebud Reservation, Oscar Micheaux (1884–1951) bought land another farmer had given up. He encouraged other African Americans to join him in South Dakota, and he wrote several books about his experience there. In 1919, Micheaux turned one of those books into a film called *The Homesteader*, the first full-length film made by an African American. He went on to create about 40 films. These movies starred black actors and were made for African American audiences. Though many of Micheaux's works have been lost, he was central in putting the African American experience on film.

? **Want to know more?** See www.naacp.org/about/history/micheaux/

A Lakota leader and medicine man is the subject of one of the largest sculptures in the state. In the Badlands, a statue of Crazy Horse is slowly being carved into a mountain. Artist Korczak Ziolkowski began the sculpture in 1948.

THE WORLD OF SPORTS

South Dakota doesn't have any major professional sports teams, but it does field teams in several minor leagues. Sioux Falls has a baseball team, the Canaries; a

The work on this Crazy Horse sculpture in the Badlands began in 1948.

A cowboy rides a bucking bronco in a rodeo in Belle Fourche.

MINI-BIO

AMANDA CLEMENT: PIONEER UMPIRE

In 1904, traveling from South Dakota to Iowa to watch her brother play baseball, Amanda Clement (1888–1971) made history. When the regular umpire didn't show up, she filled in for him and became the first professional female umpire. Clement had umpired some of her brother's games in South Dakota, and at times she also played. She went on to umpire across the Midwest, earning money to attend Yankton College. At the school, she served as a referee for basketball games, making her one of the first woman referees.

 Want to know more? See www.exploratorium. edu/baseball/clement.html

hockey team, the Stampede; and a basketball team, the Skyforce. Many sports fans in the state cheer on teams from the University of South Dakota and South Dakota State University.

One of the top sports in South Dakota traces its roots to ranching on the frontier. Rodeos feature cowboys and cowgirls riding horses, roping cattle, and racing horses around barrels. One of rodeo's greatest stars, Casey Tibbs, grew up on the frontier west of Fort Pierre. More recently, Jesse Bail from Spearfish has been a professional rodeo star. Today, rodeo is South Dakota's official state sport.

READ ABOUT

An inside look
at the dome
of the South
Dakota capitol

CHAPTER SEVEN

GOVERNMENT

★

I N SOUTH DAKOTA, PROJECT CITIZEN HELPS KIDS START LEARNING ABOUT GOVERNMENT EARLY. With the project, students study important issues and then present their views to government officials. Students in a class in Pollock studied the Missouri River reservoirs and noticed that water levels were low. The students believed that using the water for drinking should be a main priority, and they took their findings to state lawmakers. The students learned firsthand about the role all citizens can play in running a government.

The state capitol in Pierre

WORD TO KNOW

petition *a formal written request signed by a group of voters*

In 1898, South Dakota became the first state to allow voters to have their say through the initiative and referendum processes.

THE CENTER OF STATE GOVERNMENT

The center of government is in Pierre, the state capital, which sits almost exactly in the center of the state. The state legislature, the supreme court, and the governor's office are all located in the state capitol.

The details of South Dakota's government are spelled out in the state constitution. The first one was written in 1889. Changes, called amendments, have been added to the constitution over the years. Voters in South Dakota can propose both new amendments and new laws in a process called the initiative. If enough people sign a **petition**, the proposed law is placed on

Capital City

This map shows places of interest in Pierre, South Dakota's capital city.

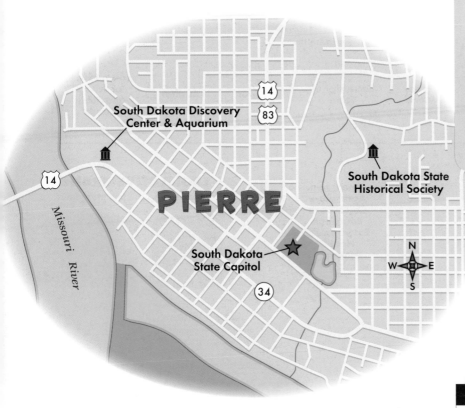

Capitol Facts

Here are some fascinating facts about South Dakota's state capitol.

Size: 292 feet (89 m) long, 190 feet (58 m) wide, 161 feet (49 m) high, with an area of more than 114,000 square feet (10,591 sq m)

Year completed: 1915; restoration done from 1975 to 1989

Cost of original building: Just under $1 million

SEE IT HERE!

THE CAPITOL

South Dakota's capitol is topped with an impressive copper dome, and visitors can explore the building every day of the year. Inside the capitol is a doll collection showing small versions of gowns worn by governors' wives. The building also has four sculptures called *Wisdom, Vision, Courage*, and *Integrity*, and paintings of goddesses from Greek mythology. On the capitol grounds are several more statues and memorials.

the ballot during an election. If more people vote for the proposed law than against it, the law is put into effect. South Dakotans can also vote to prevent a law passed by the legislature from taking effect, in a process called the referendum. Voters say yes or no to keeping the law.

LEGISLATIVE BRANCH

South Dakota's legislature includes the house of representatives and the senate. Both the house and the senate must approve a bill before it is sent to the governor to be signed into law.

South Dakota State Government

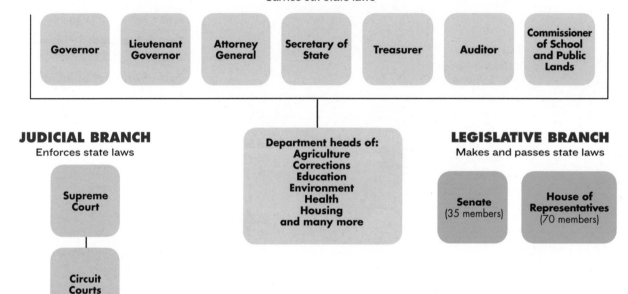

EXECUTIVE BRANCH
Carries out state laws

| Governor | Lieutenant Governor | Attorney General | Secretary of State | Treasurer | Auditor | Commissioner of School and Public Lands |

JUDICIAL BRANCH
Enforces state laws

Supreme Court

Circuit Courts

Magistrate Courts

Department heads of:
Agriculture
Corrections
Education
Environment
Health
Housing
and many more

LEGISLATIVE BRANCH
Makes and passes state laws

Senate
(35 members)

House of Representatives
(70 members)

Representing South Dakota

This list shows the number of elected officials who represent South Dakota, both on the state and national levels.

OFFICE	NUMBER	LENGTH OF TERM
State senators	35	2 years
State representatives	70	2 years
U.S. senators	2	6 years
U.S. representatives	1	2 years
Presidential electors	3	—

EXECUTIVE BRANCH

The executive branch in South Dakota includes seven positions that are chosen by voters. The most important is governor. The governor must sign a bill for it to become law. He or she may also veto it to reject it. The state legislature can override a veto if two-thirds of the members in each house vote again for the bill. As leader of the executive branch, the governor chooses people to lead various executive departments. The senate must approve most of these choices. The governor proposes a budget for the

Governor Mike Rounds prepares to sign a bill in 2006.

state, but state lawmakers have the final say on how much money is spent and where it goes. The governor can also rally lawmakers and citizens to support new ideas.

The lieutenant governor of South Dakota serves as president of the state senate but does not vote unless there is a tie. He or she also takes over if the governor leaves office. The secretary of state has duties such as running elections and registering voters. The attorney

Members of the state legislature discuss the 2007 annual budget.

general makes sure the state's laws are enforced and represents South Dakota in legal matters. The treasurer invests the state's money, while the state auditor makes sure people pay their taxes and that tax money is spent legally. The commissioner of schools and public lands watches over the money the state makes from the sale of land and its natural resources. These include oil, natural gas, and minerals. Most of the money earned from these resources goes to the state's schools.

JUDICIAL BRANCH

The most powerful court in the state is the supreme court. The governor appoints its five judges, called justices, who choose one of their own to serve as chief justice. Three years after justices are first named to the court, voters decide if they will remain on the court. Those who remain face new elections every eight years. The supreme court decides if rulings made in lower courts were legally correct. Supreme court justices also decide how the lower courts will be run, and they can give legal advice when a governor asks for it.

The circuit courts of South Dakota hear all cases involving crimes or disputes between citizens. Thirty-eight judges are elected to serve in seven circuits across the state. The chief justice of the state supreme court chooses a chief judge for each circuit. For less serious crimes and disputes, cases go to the magistrate courts.

GOVERNMENT CLOSER TO HOME

Like other states, South Dakota has lawmakers and executives who govern at the local level. South Dakota is divided into 66 counties, each with its own government. Voters elect county commissioners, who act as both the legislature and executive branch. Other elected positions include treasurer, auditor, sheriff, and state's attorney. Within each county are various cities, towns, and

MINI-BIO

JUDITH MEIERHENRY: DEDICATED JUSTICE

Judith Meierhenry (1944–) has devoted most of her adult life to serving the citizens of her home state. After graduating from the University of South Dakota in 1966, she spent several years teaching English before entering law school. She earned her law degree in 1977. In 2002, Meierhenry made history when she became the first woman named to the South Dakota Supreme Court. Since then, she has worked to educate women about the law.

 Want to know more? See www.usd.edu/law/lawrev/alumnifriends_distinguished.html

WEIRD AND WACKY LAWS

Every state has strange laws, and South Dakota is no exception. Here are two silly laws that are still on the books, but it's unlikely either is enforced these days!

- It's illegal to lie down and fall asleep in a South Dakota cheese factory.

- Movies that show police officers being mistreated are forbidden.

89

Members of the Oglala Sioux Nation perform traditional chants as former U.S. president Bill Clinton (rear center) looks on, 1999.

Want to know more? See www.sd4history.com/Unit9/benreifel.htm

MINI-BIO

BEN REIFEL: LAWMAKER

Ben Reifel (1906–1990) journeyed from a South Dakota log cabin to the U.S. Capitol. He grew up on the Rosebud Reservation, the son of a Brulé Lakota mother and German American father. After college, he worked for the U.S. Bureau of Indian Affairs. He helped Native Americans in South Dakota set up new tribal governments. In 1960, Reifel entered politics and won a seat in the U.S. House of Representatives, making him the first Sioux to serve in Congress. He worked hard for all voters in his district, Sioux and non-Indian alike, and was reelected four times.

districts. Voters elect people to serve on boards that pass **ordinances** and collect taxes. Local and county governments build schools and libraries, hire police officers, maintain roads, and provide other essential public services.

WORD TO KNOW

ordinances *laws passed by local governments*

South Dakota Counties

This map shows the 66 counties in South Dakota. Pierre, the state capital, is indicated with a star.

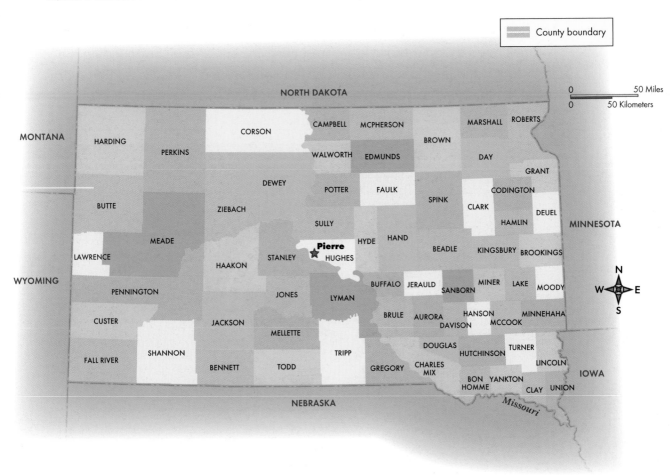

| | County boundary |

GOVERNMENT ON THE RESERVATIONS

Each of South Dakota's nine Indian tribes is its own nation with its own constitution. Voters choose their own government, made up of a tribal president (or chairperson) and council. The tribes also have their own courts. South Dakota's Office of Tribal Government Relations helps tribes pass laws that improve life on the reservations.

State Flag

The original state flag of South Dakota was designed and adopted in 1909. The flag features a field of blue with the state seal in the center. The state seal is surrounded by gold triangles representing the sun's rays. Surrounding the state seal is the inscription "South Dakota" on top and "The Mount Rushmore State" on the bottom.

State Seal

The outer ring of the seal reads "State of South Dakota" on the top and "Great Seal" on the bottom. The outer ring also features the year of statehood, 1889. Inside the inner circle of the seal is the state motto, "Under God the People Rule." At the center of the seal is an image featuring hills, a river with a boat, a farmer, a mine, and cattle. These represent the state's industrial strength and natural resources.

94

READ ABOUT

A South Dakota farmer inspects his crop of sunflowers.

CHAPTER EIGHT

ECONOMY

★

IN THE PAST, GETTING UP EARLY TO WORK THE FIELDS OR TAKE CARE OF LIVESTOCK WAS A WAY OF LIFE FOR MOST SOUTH DAKOTANS. Farming and ranching are still big business in the state, but the average worker is more likely to be found in a factory, office building, or store than on a farm. Whatever they do, South Dakotans work hard to help the state's economy grow.

A rancher rounds up a herd of cattle.

South Dakota ranks number one in the country for raising bison for their meat. State ranchers own just over 40,000 head of bison.

FARMING AND RANCHING

For decades, the number of farms in South Dakota has dropped as the size of farms has grown. Meanwhile, machinery has helped farmers grow more crops with fewer people. The crops grown have also changed. While corn and wheat are still important, soybeans and sunflowers are now also common. Corn, the top crop, brought in more than $730 million to state farmers in 2006. Soybeans were not far behind, at almost $696 million.

Ranching plays a huge part in South Dakota's farm economy as well. Raising livestock was a $2.6 billion industry in 2006, with cattle and calves the top product. South Dakota farmers also raise hogs, turkeys, sheep, and lambs. Some South Dakotans keep bees, and their honey

What Do South Dakotans Do?

This color-coded chart shows what industries South Dakotans work in.

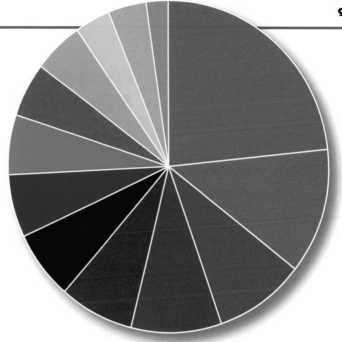

23.4% Educational services, health care, and social assistance, 78,338	**7.7%** Manufacturing, 25,909	**5.2%** Transportation, warehousing, and utilities, 17,435
	6.7% Construction, 22,357	**5.0%** Public administration, 16,874
12.4% Retail trade, 41,666	**6.1%** Professional, scientific, management, administrative, and waste management services, 20,439	**3.7%** Other services, except public administration, 12,458
9.1% Agriculture, forestry, fishing, hunting, and mining, 30,309		**3.7%** Wholesale trade, 12,391
9.0% Arts, entertainment, recreation, accommodation, and food services, 30,174	**5.8%** Finance, insurance, real estate, rental, and leasing, 19,410	**2.2%** Information, 7,250

Source: U.S. Census Bureau, 2006 estimate

is a valuable product, worth more than $8 million in 2006. The honeybee was named the state insect in 1978.

WEALTH FROM THE EARTH

Gold drew thousands of people to South Dakota's Black Hills in the 19th century, but today just one major gold mine remains open in the state. Rocks, stones, and clays used in construction are now the top nonfuel minerals produced in the state. These include Portland cement, sand and gravel, mica, and granite.

Top Products

Agriculture Cattle and calves, corn, soybeans, hogs, wheat, dairy products, hay, sunflowers

Manufacturing Food products, machinery, electric and electronics equipment

Mining Portland cement, sand and gravel, crushed stone, gold

Major Agricultural and Mining Products

This map shows where South Dakota's major agricultural and mining products come from. See a cow? That means cattle are raised there.

Urban area	
Grazing, rangeland	
Farming	
Forests, some farming	

Map legend:

Cattle		Mineral mining	
Coal		Natural gas	
Dairy		Oats	
Gold		Oil	
Grains		Poultry	
Hay		Sheep	
Hogs		Soybeans	
Manufacturing		Sunflowers	

MAKING THINGS

Many South Dakotans who have moved to the city from the countryside have taken jobs in factories. The state's largest manufacturer is John Morrell & Company, which makes pork products. Its plant in Sioux Falls employs more than 3,000 workers. Daktronics, based in Brookings, makes scoreboards and electronic signs of all shapes and sizes.

Many Native Americans earn a living by creating art related to their culture. Greg Red Elk is shown here with some of his acrylic paintings.

South Dakota is constantly recruiting new companies to come to the state. A leading business magazine named Sioux Falls as the best small city in the country for business. Others say South Dakota is the best state for entrepreneurs—people going into business for themselves. In recent years, companies that make things such as rifles and wind turbine blades have made plans to move to the state. The arrival of new companies means more jobs for construction workers. They build offices for the companies and new homes for people who work for them. More than 21,000 South Dakotans worked in construction in 2005.

SEE IT HERE!

SIOUX POTTERY

Not everything made in South Dakota comes from a farm or factory. See for yourself at Sioux Pottery in Rapid City. The artists are Lakotas. They specialize in making items out of red clay from the Black Hills. At the studio, you can meet the artists and watch them make pots, plates, Christmas ornaments, and other items.

MINI-BIO

ERNEST LAWRENCE: PRIZE-WINNING SCIENTIST

Physicist Ernest Lawrence (1901–1958) was born in Canton and graduated from the University of South Dakota in 1922. In 1930, he created the cyclotron, a circular device that speeds the movement of tiny particles of matter. The cyclotron helped Lawrence and other scientists study the tiniest particles known, and doctors have used beams of energy created by cyclotrons to treat cancer. For his work, Lawrence received science's highest award, the Nobel Prize in Physics. He is the only Nobel winner from South Dakota.

 Want to know more? See http://nobelprize.org/nobel_prizes/physics/laureates/1939/lawrence-bio.html

WORD TO KNOW

physics *the study of matter and energy*

Homestake Gold Mine is the deepest mine in the Western Hemisphere, plunging more than 8,000 feet (2,438 m) underground.

Making new products often requires scientists and engineers to do research. In 2007, the National Science Foundation chose South Dakota as the site of its new laboratory, the Deep Underground Science and Engineering Laboratory, which will be the world's deepest laboratory. In the old Homestake Gold Mine in Lead, scientists will conduct **physics** experiments and study life-forms that live deep below the earth.

SERVING OTHERS

Banking, selling goods, government work, and health care are just some parts of South Dakota's service economy. When it comes to putting people to work, the government is close to the top. More than 69,000 people work for some level of government in South Dakota—local, county, state, federal, or tribal. Government jobs are especially important on Indian reservations.

Health care is a growing field in South Dakota, and Sanford Health is the largest nongovernment employer in the state, with more than 5,000 workers. The largest part of the service economy in South Dakota is tied to selling goods. Another important service is helping people take care of their money. Several large U.S. banks have operations in Sioux Falls that process credit card accounts for their customers.

Another service involves taking care of the several million tourists who visit South Dakota each year. In

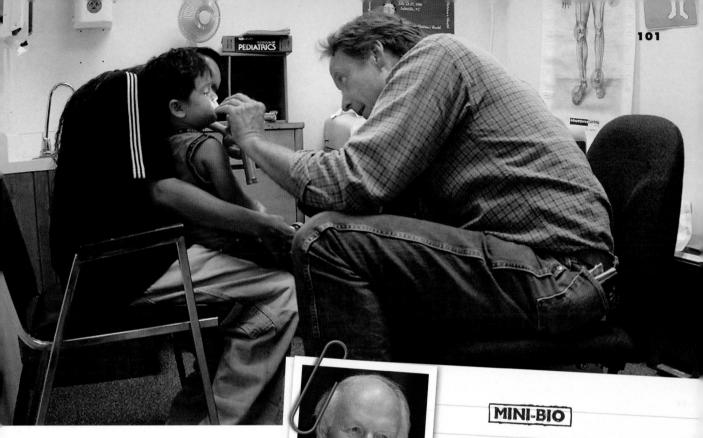

A doctor on the Pine Ridge Indian Reservation gives an Oglala Sioux boy a checkup.

2006, those guests spent more than $860 million, money that helped create jobs for almost 34,000 tour guides, chefs, hotel workers, and others. Many tourists come to hunt and fish. Visitors also spend money on Indian reservations. Some come to enjoy nature, while others go to tribal casinos. Tourism money helps reservation governments provide people with services.

MINI-BIO

T. DENNY SANFORD: BIG-TIME GIVER

As a young boy, T. Denny Sanford (1935–) got his first taste of the business world in his father's clothing company. After graduating from college in 1958, he started his own company, which sold construction products, and he later bought a chemical company.

In 1986, Sanford bought the United National Bank of Sioux Falls (now called First Premier Bank). In recent years, he has made many large donations to South Dakota organizations. The biggest came in 2007, when he gave $400 million to the Sioux Valley Hospitals and Health System. The company was renamed Sanford Health in his honor.

❓ **Want to know more?** See www.philanthropy.com/free/articles/v19/i08/08000701.htm

NORTH DAKOTA

MONTANA

N
W E
S

Lemmon
Grand
Standing Rock Reservation
Kenel
Mobridge
Aberdeen

Sisseton
Eden
Roslyn
Waubay
Red

MINNESOTA

29

Milbank

Moreau

Castle Rock
Eagle Butte
Lake Oahe
Gettysburg
Watertown
Clear Lake

Belle Fourche
Redfield
Miller
Big Sioux

Spearfish
Belle Fourche
Cheyenne
Brookings

Deadwood
Lead
Sturgis
Rapid City
Geographic Center of South Dakota
De Smet
Flandrea

WYOMING

Pierre
Missouri
Bad
Huron
Madison

Black Hills National Forest
Wall
Philip
Murdo
Lake Sharpe
James
Dell Rapids
Brandon

Keystone
Custer
Chamberlain
Mitchell
Sioux Falls
229

Hot Springs
Interior
White
90
90
29

Badlands National Park
Mission
Winner
Lake Francis Case
Pickstown
Yankton
Vermillion
IOWA

N. Sioux City

90   Interstate highway

0   50 Miles
0   50 Kilometers

NEBRASKA

TRAVEL GUIDE

★

WHETHER YOU HEAD TO EAST RIVER OR WEST RIVER, YOU'LL FIND PLENTY TO SEE AND DO IN SOUTH DAKOTA. Natural beauty calls throughout the Black Hills, and museums display the talents of some of the state's best artists. Meanwhile, sites in Deadwood and elsewhere allow you to step into the state's past. With so much to see, you'll learn why some folks call South Dakota the Land of Infinite Variety!

← Follow along with this travel map. We'll start our trip in Sioux Falls and end in Lemmon!

SOUTHEAST

THINGS TO DO: Take a musical trip through time, see Native American art, and go for a swim in Lewis and Clark Lake.

Sioux Falls

★ **Washington Pavilion of Arts and Science:** This facility includes a theater that features concerts and plays, a museum with all sorts of art, and the Kirby Science Discovery Center, where kids can learn about lasers, dinosaurs, weather, and much more.

★ **Great Plains Zoo:** More than 500 animals from around the world make their home at the Great Plains Zoo. They include wallabies from Australia, giraffes from Africa, and tortoises from South America. The zoo also has a natural history museum.

Feeding the goats at Great Plains Zoo

★ **Center for Western Studies:** Located at Augustana College, this center traces the history of the plains, from the Native American nations to Yankee and immigrant settlers. Displays range from Sioux clothing to furniture made by Norwegian immigrants.

★ **Falls Park:** At the center of this park are the waterfalls that gave Sioux Falls its name. A tower in the park gives a good view of the region, and you can walk along the remains of an old mill that was once powered by the rushing waters.

★ **USS *South Dakota* Battleship Memorial:** During World War II, sailors onboard the *South Dakota* fought all over the Pacific Ocean. Today, parts of the historic ship are on display at this memorial in Sherman Park. See for yourself just how big a 94-ton gun barrel is!

★ **Northern Plains Tribal Arts Festival:** For several days in September, Sioux Falls is home to a celebration of Native American art from across the Great Plains. Artists from 33 tribes display beadwork, paintings, and more. Saturday night features a powwow with dancing and drumming.

Lewis and Clark Recreation Area

Yankton

★ **Lewis and Clark Recreation Area:** Just outside of Yankton is Lewis and Clark Lake. At 22 miles (35 km) long, the lake offers plenty of water for boaters and swimmers. Around the lake are golf courses, campgrounds, bike trails, horse grounds—even an archery course.

★ **African Methodist Episcopal Church:** The first black church in Dakota Territory, this church is still being used today.

Mitchell

★ **Dakota Discovery Museum:** This museum displays a real bison skin tipi and a cabin like the ones homesteaders built to claim their own piece of South Dakota land. The museum also has works by Oscar Howe, Harvey Dunn, and other notable South Dakota artists.

SEE IT HERE!

NATIONAL MUSIC MUSEUM

At the National Music Museum, you won't just see it here—you'll hear it, too! As you walk among the hundreds of instruments, you can listen to a recording of some of them being played. Museum displays range from Asian flutes to electric guitars, and some of the instruments are hundreds of years old. Seeing them, you realize instruments can be beautiful works of art as well as tools to make equally beautiful music.

Guitars at the National Music Museum

★ **Enchanted World Doll Museum:** Inside this museum, which looks like a castle, are almost 5,000 dolls, some dating to the 1800s, and from more than 120 countries.

Vermillion

★ **W. H. Over Museum of Natural and Cultural History:** This museum includes displays about Native American and pioneer life and the natural history of South Dakota.

Pickstown

★ **Fort Randall Dam and Historic Site:** The Fort Randall Dam is one of several dams providing power to South Dakotans. You can tour the power plant and explore the nearby Fort Randall Historic Site. On the site are the remains of the army fort built there in 1856.

NORTHEAST

THINGS TO DO: Sample some sour food, imagine what it was like to be a pioneer child, and see thousands of birds at a wildlife refuge.

Brookings

★ **South Dakota Art Museum:** South Dakota's major art museum houses a large collection of works by Native American artists and painter Harvey Dunn. At the museum's Kids Sensation Station, young visitors can explore their own artistic talents.

Eden

★ **Fort Sisseton State Historical Park:** In pioneer days, soldiers at Fort Sisseton helped keep the peace between Native Americans and white settlers. Today, the

MINI-BIO

LAWRENCE DIGGS: THE VINEGAR MAN

At a tiny museum in Roslyn, near Eden, Lawrence Diggs (1948–) tells the world about the wonders of vinegar. Before coming to South Dakota, Diggs lived on several continents and served in the Peace Corps, which sends American volunteers to developing countries. He decided the small town of Roslyn was the perfect spot for a museum devoted to his favorite sour liquid. He studied how to make vinegar and cook with it. At his museum, Diggs shares his knowledge and displays paper made from vinegar.

? Want to know more? See www.vinegarman.com/Vinegarman.shtml

remains of the fort give a glimpse into South Dakota's history. Many of the original buildings have been preserved or rebuilt, and guides dressed as 19th-century soldiers offer tours.

Soldiers reenacting daily life at Fort Sisseton

Ingalls Home & Museum

De Smet

★ **Ingalls Home & Museum:** Laura Ingalls Wilder wrote about her family's experiences on the South Dakota prairie. At this site, visitors can relive some of those experiences by exploring a dugout—a simple home built partially in the earth—or taking a ride in a covered wagon. There are also life-size models of the home and barn the Ingalls family built during the 1880s.

Waubay

★ **Waubay National Wildlife Refuge:** *Waubay* is Sioux for "a nesting place for birds." Today, about 100 kinds of birds nest in the refuge, and more than 240 species of birds spend at least part of the year there. They're attracted to habitats that range from forests to marshlands to prairie grasses.

Aberdeen

★ **Wylie Park:** This park includes typical activities such as camping, hiking, and sports. It also has a yellow brick road and people dressed as characters from *The Wizard of Oz.* Storybook Land features scenes from well-known folktales and songs, such as "There Was an Old Woman Who Lived in a Shoe" and "Jack and Jill."

★ **Dacotah Prairie Museum:** What's an elephant doing on the prairie? Amazing the visitors who come to this museum! The 11-foot-tall (3.4 m) beast is the largest of more than 50 mounted animals on display here. Others include a polar bear and a zebra. The museum also has exhibits on South Dakota art and history.

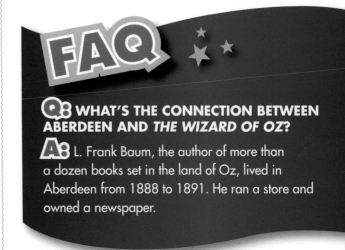

FAQ

Q8 WHAT'S THE CONNECTION BETWEEN ABERDEEN AND *THE WIZARD OF OZ*?

A8 L. Frank Baum, the author of more than a dozen books set in the land of Oz, lived in Aberdeen from 1888 to 1891. He ran a store and owned a newspaper.

CENTRAL SOUTH DAKOTA

THINGS TO DO: Learn more about some great South Dakotans, get your hands on a real bison hide, and admire Lakota art.

Chamberlain

★ **South Dakota Hall of Fame:** This museum highlights South Dakotans who made their mark in politics, sports, education, business, the arts, and other fields.

★ **Akta Lakota Museum & Cultural Center:** On the grounds of the St. Joseph Indian School is this museum dedicated to Lakota history. From life on the plains before Europeans arrived through today's efforts to preserve traditional culture, you'll learn it all here.

Akta Lakota Museum & Cultural Center

Medicine Rock at Dakota Sunset Museum

Gettysburg

★ **Dakota Sunset Museum:** This museum is the home of one big rock—it weighs about 40 tons. The big stone is called Medicine Rock. Several footprints are embedded in the rock, and no one is sure how they got there. The museum also has an old-time blacksmith shop.

Pierre

★ **South Dakota Discovery Center & Aquarium:** For hands-on science fun, the Discovery Center is the place to go. Kids can crawl through a life-size dinosaur nest or learn how to use lab equipment at the Imagination Station. The aquarium features fish found in the nearby Missouri River.

★ **Lake Oahe:** This lake was created when a dam was built along the Missouri River. Lake Oahe stretches out for 250 miles (402 km), providing plenty of recreational activities. Fishing is a major sport, with walleye the main catch.

★ **Lewis and Clark Family Center:** Located at the Farm Island Recreation Area, this center is full of hands-on fun. Feel real elk and bison skins, or sit inside a dugout canoe, the kind used by Indians and trappers centuries ago. You can also learn more about the experiences of Lewis and Clark as they traveled through South Dakota.

SEE IT HERE!

CULTURAL HERITAGE CENTER

Want to explore all of South Dakota's history in one spot? Then the state historical society's Cultural Heritage Center in Pierre is the place to go. The museum is the largest in the state and features more than 1,300 items relating to Sioux history—including a life-size tipi. You can also see a life-size sod house and exhibits and documents describing South Dakota from settler days to the present.

Mobridge

★ **Klein Museum:** Step into the old country schoolhouse at this museum—just one sample of life on the frontier in pioneer days. The museum also has examples of Lakota art.

Standing Rock Reservation

★ **Sitting Bull and Sacagawea Monuments:** Overlooking the Missouri River is a marker showing the spot where the great Lakota chief Sitting Bull is said to be buried. South Dakota artist Korczak Ziolkowski created the sculpture of the chief's head that tops the marker. Another monument nearby honors Sacagawea, the Shoshone woman who traveled with Lewis and Clark on their expedition.

Sitting Bull monument and grave site

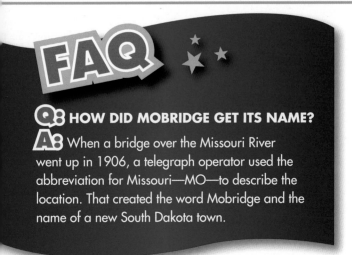

FAQ

Q8 HOW DID MOBRIDGE GET ITS NAME?

A8 When a bridge over the Missouri River went up in 1906, a telegraph operator used the abbreviation for Missouri—MO—to describe the location. That created the word Mobridge and the name of a new South Dakota town.

Kenel

★ **Fort Manuel Lisa:** Manuel Lisa helped create South Dakota's fur trade, and the fort named for him is a life-size model of the one he built outside Kenel in 1811. According to some reports, Sacagawea died at about age 25 at the original fort; the new one has an exhibit about her life.

Murdo

★ **Pioneer Auto Museum and Antique Town:** Want to see one of the world's few eight-wheeled cars? Then head to this museum, which has about 250 cars, trucks, and motorcycles—some more than 100 years old. Other collections include pedal cars, toys, bikes— even doorknobs!

THE BADLANDS AND THE BLACK HILLS

THINGS TO DO: Get close to some big bones, take an elevator ride underground, and journey into the past.

Mission

★ **Sicangu Heritage Center:** On the Rosebud Sioux Reservation, this museum tracks the history of the Sicangu (Brulé) Lakota. The exhibits include quilts and spectacular feather headdresses.

Interior

★ **Badlands National Park:** Covering 381 square miles (987 sq km), this national park features some of the most colorful eroded hills and gullies of the Badlands region. Hikers might see bison, bighorn sheep, or swift foxes.

Badlands National Park

Philip

★ **Minuteman Missile National Historic Site:** Take an elevator ride underground to see where members of the U.S. Air Force once sat ready in case they ever got an order to fire missiles. The Minuteman site traces the role South Dakota played during the cold war.

Sturgis

★ **Motorcycle Museum & Hall of Fame:** Since 2001, Sturgis has been home to the Motorcycle Museum & Hall of Fame, which displays some motorcycles that are more than 100 years old.

Deadwood

★ **Days of '76 Museum:** This museum honors the Days of '76 Rodeo, which has been held since 1923. Real stagecoaches and horse-drawn carriages are on display, along with photos from the rodeos.

★ **Tatanka—Story of the Bison:** At the heart of this site is a series of large sculptures showing three Native Americans on horseback hunting 14 bison. The site also has a tipi and Lakotas in traditional clothing who explain their people's long relationship with bison.

Adams Museum

★ **Adams Museum:** The oldest museum in the Black Hills features a copy of the gold nugget—found by local legend "Potato Creek" Johnny—said to be one of the largest ever uncovered in the area. The real nugget, weighing just under 8 ounces (227 grams), is locked up in the museum. You can also see guns that once belonged to Wild Bill Hickok.

Rapid City

★ **The Journey Museum:** Take a journey to the past, when dinosaurs once roamed the Black Hills. The museum traces the region's history from those ancient days right up to the present.

An albino python at Reptile Gardens

★ **Reptile Gardens:** This site is home to the largest reptile collection in the world. From huge alligators to deadly snakes, they're all here.

★ **South Dakota Air and Space Museum:** Located on the Ellsworth Air Force Base, this museum lets you get close to some of the best fighter planes ever flown. You can even feel what it's like to fly some of these jets!

Lead

★ **Black Hills Mining Museum:** Get your hands wet, just like the miners of old, at this museum. You can pan for tiny nuggets of gold as well as learn about the history of mining in the Black Hills.

Wall

★ **Wounded Knee Museum:** The museum covers this painful part of Lakota history in great detail, from the arrival of the Ghost Dancers to the massacre itself.

SEE IT HERE!

WALL DRUG

A stuffed jackrabbit topped with antelope horns—South Dakotans call it a jackalope—is just one of the odd items for sale at Wall Drug. What once was a tiny drugstore has grown into a major tourist stop, thanks to humorous signs for the store posted all over South Dakota. The first signs for Wall Drug offered free cold water to anyone who came by. Today, the store is famous for its homemade doughnuts and robotic singing cowboys, as well as souvenirs of all kinds.

Spearfish

★ **D. C. Booth National Historic Fish Hatchery:** This **hatchery** is one of the oldest in the country. It features a museum and an underwater viewing area where visitors can see some of the fish hatched there.

WORD TO KNOW

hatchery *a place where eggs of fish or other animals are hatched in large numbers*

Custer

★ **Black Hills National Forest:** This national forest is more than just trees. It also has caves, lakes, grasslands, and mountains. South Dakota's highest spot, Harney Peak, is in the forest, and a tower on top of it offers a view of neighboring states, as well as the Black Hills themselves.

★ **Homestake Mine Tour:** Gold made Lead a boomtown, and today, you can visit sites where gold was once processed. At the end of your visit, you'll get your own small nugget of gold taken from local mines.

Bighorn sheep at Custer State Park

★ **Custer State Park:** About 1,500 bison roam this state park, along with pronghorn, bighorn sheep, and mountain goats. The park offers miles of trails and beautiful camping sites, as well as five lakes. Rock climbers come to scale the Needles, long, thin columns of granite that shoot up from the forests.

★ **Crazy Horse Memorial:** Since 1948, workers have been carving a huge statue of the Lakota leader Crazy Horse in the Black Hills, just north of Custer. Today, the face is complete, and work continues on his long, outstretched arm. The site also has a museum and cultural center where you can learn more about Native American history.

★ **Four Mile Old West Town:**
Stagecoaches once stopped at
this spot 4 miles (6 km) outside
of Custer, which led to its name.
Today, Four Mile shows what a typical frontier town looked like, with
its saloon, general store, and jails.
You can still see some grooves cut
into the ground by horse-drawn
wagons. Actors play the part of
original settlers and help explain
the history of Four Mile.

Hot Springs

★ **Wind Cave National Park:** More
than 100 miles (160 km) of underground caves and passages are at
the heart of this national park.

★ **Black Hills Wild Horse
Sanctuary:** Just outside of Hot
Springs, herds of wild horses roam
freely, as they did across the Great
Plains hundreds of years ago.
Visitors can see ancient Native
American rock carvings.

Mustangs at Black Hills Wild Horse Sanctuary

SEE IT HERE!

MAMMOTH SITE MUSEUM

More than 25,000 years ago, the Black Hills were home
to mammoths, relatives of today's elephants. Today,
at this site in Hot Springs, archaeologists still work to
uncover the bones of these creatures, which grew to a
height of 14 feet (4.3 m). The remains of 55 mammoths
have been found. Visitors can walk among the partially
uncovered bones, or head into the exhibition hall to see
a life-size model of a complete mammoth.

★ **Jewel Cave National Monument:**
At just over 141 miles (227 km),
Jewel is the third-longest cave in
the world. Visitors can explore
part of the cave and learn about its
crystals and other rock formations.

Keystone

★ **National Presidential Wax
Museum:** All the U.S. presidents—
or at least wax versions of them
—are in Keystone. These life-size
sculptures depict the leaders in
historic scenes, and recordings
provide details about their lives.

★ **Mount Rushmore National
Memorial:** This massive granite
sculpture, near Keystone, features four U.S. presidents: George

Mount Rushmore National Memorial

Washington, Thomas Jefferson, Theodore Roosevelt, and Abraham Lincoln. More than 2.5 million people visit the site each year.

★ **Borglum Historical Center:** Gutzon Borglum won acclaim for creating Mount Rushmore; this center gives the complete story of his life and art.

NORTHWEST CORNER

THINGS TO DO: See wood that has turned to rock or learn about rodeos.

Belle Fourche

★ **Tri-State Museum:** This museum honors the shared history of South Dakota and the neighboring parts of Wyoming and Montana. The focus is on pioneer days and rodeos.

★ **Center of the Nation Monument:** When Alaska and Hawai'i entered the United States in 1959, the geographic center of the country shifted to a site within South Dakota. In 2007, Belle Fourche officials put down a huge concrete and bronze monument to mark that honor. The actual spot is about 20 miles (32 km) north of Belle Fourche on old Highway 85. A small marker there shows the U.S. government's best guess of the exact center.

Lemmon

★ **Petrified Wood Park and Museum:** Petrified wood is ancient wood that has turned rock-hard over time. Lemmon claims to have the world's largest park and museum devoted to petrified wood. One of the attractions is a giant castle made of petrified wood and petrified dinosaur and mammoth bones.

★ **Grand River Museum:** There's a little something for everyone at this museum, from dinosaur bones to exhibits on ranching to the giant sculptures that local artist John Lopez made from scrap metal. Sitting Bull and a *T. rex* are just two of the subjects Lopez captured in metal.

WRITING PROJECTS

Check out these ideas for creating a campaign brochure and writing you-are-there narratives. Or research the lives of famous people from South Dakota.

118

ART PROJECTS

You can illustrate the state song, create a dazzling PowerPoint presentation, or learn about the state quarter and design your own.

119

TIMELINE

What happened when? This timeline highlights important events in the state's history—and shows what was happening throughout the United States at the same time.

122

FAST FACTS

Use this section to find fascinating facts about state symbols, land area and population statistics, weather, sports teams, and much more.

126

GLOSSARY

Remember the Words to Know from the chapters in this book? They're all collected here.

125

SCIENCE, TECHNOLOGY, & MATH PROJECTS

Make weather maps, graph population statistics, and research endangered species that live in the state.

120

PRIMARY VS. SECONDARY SOURCES

121

So what are primary and secondary sources? And what's the diff? This section explains all that and where you can find them.

BIOGRAPHICAL DICTIONARY

133

This at-a-glance guide highlights some of the state's most important and influential people. Visit this section and read about their contributions to the state, the country, and the world.

RESOURCES

Books, Web sites, DVDs, and more. Take a look at these additional sources for information about the state.

137

WRITING PROJECTS

★ ★ ★

Write a Memoir, Journal, or Editorial for Your School Newspaper!

Picture Yourself . . .

★ As a child growing up in a Lakota camp. How would your responsibilities change and expand as you grow older? Would there be different responsibilities for boys and girls? What would everyday life be like?

SEE: Chapter Two, page 30.

GO TO: www.bigorrin.org/lakota_kids.htm

★ Moving with your family to the South Dakota prairie. Write journal entries describing what life is like. How do you build a sod house? Where do you find food? How do you keep warm?

SEE: Chapter Four, pages 50–52.

GO TO: www.museumoftheamericanwest.org/explore/exhibits/sod/daily.html

Create an Election Brochure or Web Site!

Run for office! Throughout this book, you've read about some of the issues that concern South Dakota today. As a candidate for governor of South Dakota, create a campaign brochure or Web site.

★ Explain how you meet the qualifications to be governor of South Dakota.

★ Talk about the three or four major issues you'll focus on if you're elected.

★ Remember, you'll be responsible for South Dakota's budget. How would you spend the taxpayers' money?

SEE: Chapter Seven, pages 86–88.

GO TO: South Dakota's Government Web site at www.sd.gov. You might also want to read some local newspapers. Try these:

Argus Leader (Sioux Falls) at www.argusleader.com

Rapid City Journal at www.rapidcityjournal.com

Create an interview script with a famous person from South Dakota!

★ Research various South Dakotans, such as Sitting Bull, Mamie Shields Pyle, Joe Foss, Russell Means, Laura Ingalls Wilder, Oscar Howe, Oscar Micheaux, Amanda Clement, Tom Brokaw, Mary Hart, and others.

★ Based on your research, pick one person you would most like to talk with.

★ Write a script of the interview. What questions would you ask? How would this person answer? Create a question-and-answer format. You may want to supplement this writing project with a voice-recording dramatization of the interview.

SEE: Chapters Four, Five, and Six, pages 48, 56, 63, 66, 78, 79, 80, 81, and the Biographical Dictionary, pages 133–136.

GO TO: www.sdhalloffame.com/specials.cfm?cat_id=15

ART PROJECTS

Create a PowerPoint Presentation or Visitors' Guide
Welcome to South Dakota!

South Dakota's a great place to visit and to live! From its natural beauty to its historical sites, there's plenty to see and do. In your PowerPoint presentation or brochure, highlight 10 to 15 of South Dakota's fascinating landmarks. Be sure to include:

★ a map of the state showing where these sites are located

★ photos, illustrations, Web links, natural history facts, geographic stats, climate and weather, plants and wildlife, and recent discoveries

SEE: Chapter Nine, pages 102–115, and Fast Facts, pages 126–127.

GO TO: The official tourism Web site for South Dakota at www.travelsd.com. Download and print maps, photos, and vacation ideas for tourists.

Illustrate the Lyrics to the South Dakota State Song
("Hail! South Dakota")

Use markers, paints, photos, collages, colored pencils, or computer graphics to illustrate the lyrics to "Hail! South Dakota." Turn your illustrations into a picture book, or scan them into PowerPoint and add music.

SEE: The lyrics to "Hail! South Dakota" on page 128.

GO TO: The South Dakota state government Web site at www.sd.gov to find out more about the origin of the state song.

State Quarter Project

From 1999 to 2008, the U.S. Mint introduced new quarters commemorating each of the 50 states in the order that they were admitted to the Union. Each state's quarter features a unique design on its back, or reverse.

GO TO: www.usmint.gov/kids and find out what's featured on the back of the South Dakota quarter.

★ Research the significance of the image. Who designed the quarter? Who chose the final design?

★ Design your own South Dakota quarter. What images would you choose for the reverse?

★ Make a poster showing the South Dakota quarter and label each image.

SCIENCE, TECHNOLOGY, & MATH PROJECTS

★ ★ ★

Graph Population Statistics!

★ Compare population statistics (such as ethnic background, birth, death, and literacy rates) in South Dakota counties or major cities. In your graph or chart, look at population density and write sentences describing what the population statistics show; graph one set of population statistics and write a paragraph explaining what the graphs reveal.

SEE: Chapter Six, pages 72–75.

GO TO: The official Web site for the U.S. Census Bureau at www.census.gov and at http://quickfacts.census.gov/qfd/states/46000.html to find out more about population statistics, how they work, and what the statistics are for South Dakota.

Create a Weather Map of South Dakota!

Use your knowledge of South Dakota geography to research and identify conditions that result in specific weather events. What is it about the geography of South Dakota that makes it vulnerable to things like blizzards? Create a weather map or poster that shows the weather patterns over the state. Include a caption explaining the technology used to measure weather phenomena and provide data.

SEE: Chapter One, pages 15–16.

GO TO: The National Oceanic and Atmospheric Administration's National Weather Service Web site at www.weather.gov for weather maps and forecasts for South Dakota.

Whooping crane

Track Endangered Species

Using your knowledge of South Dakota's wildlife, research which animals and plants are endangered or threatened.

★ Find out what the state is doing to protect these species.

★ Chart known populations of the animals and plants, and report on changes in certain geographic areas.

SEE: Chapter One, page 19.

GO TO: Web sites such as www.sdconservation.org/wildlife/endangered.html for lists of endangered species in South Dakota.

PRIMARY VS. SECONDARY SOURCES

★ ★ ★

What's the Diff?

Your teacher may require at least one or two primary sources and one or two secondary sources for your assignment. So, what's the difference between the two?

★ **Primary sources are original.** You are reading the actual words of someone's diary, journal, letter, autobiography, or interview. Primary sources can also be photographs, maps, prints, cartoons, news/film footage, posters, first-person newspaper articles, drawings, musical scores, and recordings. By the way, when you conduct a survey, interview someone, shoot a video, or take photographs to include in a project, you are creating primary sources!

★ **Secondary sources are what you find in encyclopedias, textbooks, articles, biographies, and almanacs.** These are written by a person or group of people who tell about something that happened to someone else. Secondary sources also recount what another person said or did. This book is an example of a secondary source.

Now that you know what primary sources are—where can you find them?

★ **Your school or local library:** Check the library catalog for collections of original writings, government documents, musical scores, and so on. Some of this material may be stored on microfilm. The Library of Congress Web site (www.loc.gov) is an excellent online resource for primary source materials.

★ **Historical societies:** These organizations keep historical documents, photographs, and other materials. Staff members can help you find what you are looking for. History museums are also great places to see primary sources firsthand.

★ **The Internet:** There are lots of sites that have primary sources you can download and use in a project or assignment.

TIMELINE

★ ★ ★

U.S. Events | c. 10,000 BCE | **South Dakota Events**

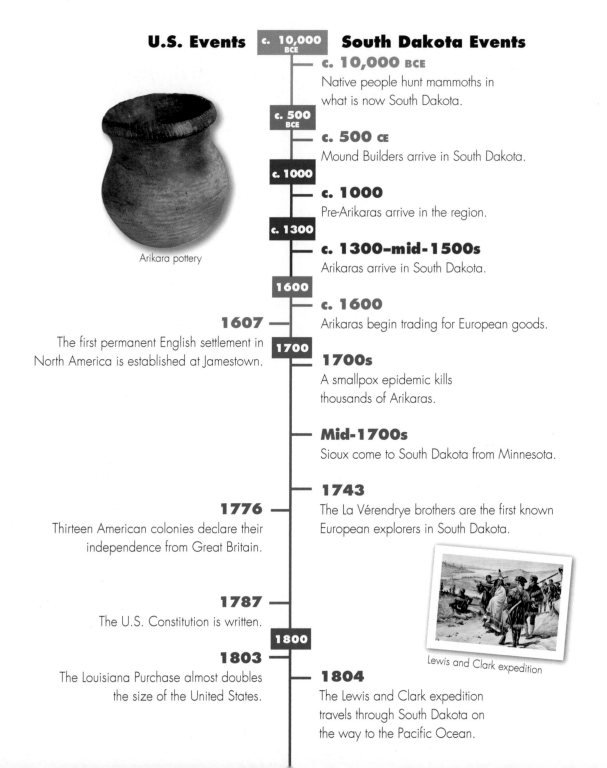

c. 10,000 BCE
Native people hunt mammoths in what is now South Dakota.

c. 500 BCE

c. 500 CE
Mound Builders arrive in South Dakota.

c. 1000

c. 1000
Pre-Arikaras arrive in the region.

c. 1300

c. 1300–mid-1500s
Arikaras arrive in South Dakota.

1600

c. 1600
Arikaras begin trading for European goods.

1607
The first permanent English settlement in North America is established at Jamestown.

1700

1700s
A smallpox epidemic kills thousands of Arikaras.

Mid-1700s
Sioux come to South Dakota from Minnesota.

1743
The La Vérendrye brothers are the first known European explorers in South Dakota.

1776
Thirteen American colonies declare their independence from Great Britain.

Arikara pottery

1787
The U.S. Constitution is written.

1800

1803
The Louisiana Purchase almost doubles the size of the United States.

Lewis and Clark expedition

1804
The Lewis and Clark expedition travels through South Dakota on the way to the Pacific Ocean.

U.S. Events

1812–15
The United States and Great Britain fight the War of 1812.

1830
The Indian Removal Act forces eastern Native American groups to relocate west of the Mississippi River.

1861–65
The American Civil War is fought between the Northern Union and the Southern Confederacy; it ends with the surrender of the Confederate army, led by General Robert E. Lee.

1886
Apache leader Geronimo surrenders to the U.S. Army, ending the last major Native American rebellion against the expansion of the United States into the West.

1900

1917–18
The United States engages in World War I.

1920
The Nineteenth Amendment to the U.S. Constitution grants women the right to vote.

South Dakota Events

Early 1800s
The fur trade thrives in South Dakota.

1851
Lakotas and other Great Plains nations sign a treaty promising peaceful relations.

1857
Sioux Falls, the first permanent European American town in South Dakota, is founded.

1861
The U.S. government creates the Dakota Territory.

1874
George Custer leads a military expedition that finds gold in the Black Hills.

1876
Lakotas fight to defend their lands.

1878–87
Thousands of homesteaders claim land during the Dakota land boom.

1889
South Dakota becomes the 40th state.

1890
U.S. troops kill about 350 Lakotas at the Wounded Knee Massacre.

Wounded Knee Massacre

U.S. Events `1900` **South Dakota Events**

1929

The stock market crashes, plunging the United States more deeply into the Great Depression.

1933

New Deal programs begin helping South Dakotans during the Great Depression.

1941–45

The United States engages in World War II.

1941–45

Thousands of South Dakotans, including Sioux code talkers, fight in World War II.

1946

Work begins on four dams across the Missouri River.

1951–53

The United States engages in the Korean War.

1964–73

The United States engages in the Vietnam War.

1973

Law officials and Native Americans clash at Wounded Knee.

1979

Lakotas are awarded more than $100 million for the loss of their lands in the Black Hills but refuse to take it.

1980s

Sioux Falls emerges as a banking center.

1991

The United States and other nations engage in the brief Persian Gulf War against Iraq.

`2000`

2001

Terrorists attack the United States on September 11.

2003

The United States and coalition forces invade Iraq.

2007

The National Science Foundation chooses the Homestake Gold Mine as the site of the Deep Underground Science and Engineering Laboratory.

2008

The United States elects its first African American president, Barack Obama.

GLOSSARY

allies people who are on the same side in a conflict

anthropologist a person who studies the development of human cultures

archaeologists people who study the remains of past human societies

constitution a written document that contains all the governing principles of a state or country

endangered at risk of becoming extinct

erosion the wearing away of land by water, ice, wind, and other factors

expedition a trip for the purpose of exploration

glaciers slow-moving masses of ice

hatchery a place where eggs of fish or other animals are hatched in large numbers

irrigation watering land by artificial means to promote plant growth

missionary a person who tries to convert others to a religion

naturalist a person who studies natural history

ordinances laws passed by local governments

petition a formal written request signed by a group of voters

physics the study of matter and energy

plateau an elevated part of the earth with steep slopes

precipitation all water that falls to the earth, including rain, sleet, hail, snow, dew, fog, or mist

refugees people who flee their homelands because of war or natural disasters

reservoirs artificial lakes or tanks for storing water

Scandinavia a region of northern Europe made up of Sweden, Norway, Denmark, Finland, and Iceland

shelterbelts rows of trees that provide shelter from the wind

sod soil thickly packed together with grass and roots

turbines machines for making power through the rotation of blades powered by wind, water, or steam

FAST FACTS

★ ★ ★

State Symbols

State seal

Statehood date	November 2, 1889, the 40th state
Origin of state name	From the Sioux word for "friend"
State capital	Pierre
State nickname	Coyote State, Mount Rushmore State
State motto	"Under God the People Rule"
State bird	Ring-necked pheasant
State flower	American pasque
State grass	Western wheatgrass
State soil	Houdek soil
State animal	Coyote
State fish	Walleye
State insect	Honeybee
State fossil	Triceratops
State mineral	Rose quartz
State gemstone	Fairburn agate
State jewelry	Black Hills gold
State song	"Hail! South Dakota"
State tree	Black Hills spruce
State fair	Late August–September at Huron

Geography

Total area; rank	77,117 square miles (199,732 sq km); 17th
Land; rank	75,885 square miles (196,541 sq km); 16th
Water; rank	1,232 square miles (3,191 sq km); 29th
Inland water; rank	1,232 square miles (3,191 sq km); 16th
Geographic center	Hughes, 8 miles (13 km) northeast of Pierre
Latitude	42°29'30'' N to 45°56' N
Longitude	98°28'33'' W to 104°3' W
Highest point	Harney Peak, 7,242 feet (2,207 m), in Pennington County
Lowest point	Big Stone Lake, 966 feet (294 m), in Roberts County

Largest city Sioux Falls
Number of counties 66
Longest river Missouri River

Population

Population; rank (2007 estimate) 796,214; 46th
Density (2007 estimate) 11 persons per square mile (4 per sq km)
Population distribution (2000 census) 52% urban, 48% rural
Race (2007 estimate) White persons: 88.4%*
American Indian and Alaska Native persons: 8.3%*
Black persons: 1.1%*
Asian persons: 0.8%*
Native Hawaiian and Other Pacific Islanders: 0.05%*
Persons reporting two or more races: 1.4%
Persons of Hispanic or Latino origin: 2.3%†
White persons not Hispanic: 86.4%

Includes persons reporting only one race.
†*Hispanics may be of any race, so they are also included in applicable race categories.*

Weather

Record high temperature 120°F (49°C) at Gann Valley on July 5, 1936
Record low temperature −58°F (−50°C) at McIntosh on February 17, 1936
Average July temperature 72°F (22°C)
Average January temperature 22°F (−6°C)
Average yearly precipitation 16 inches (41 cm)

State flag

STATE SONG

★ ★ ★

"Hail! South Dakota"

DeeCort Hammitt wrote the words and music to this march. It officially became the state song in 1943.

Hail! South Dakota, A great state of the land,
Health, wealth and beauty, That's what makes her grand;
She has her Black Hills, And mines with gold so rare,
And with her scenery, No other state can compare.

Come where the sun shines, And where life's worth your while,
You won't be here long, 'Till you'll wear a smile;
No state's so healthy, And no folk quite so true,
To South Dakota. We welcome you.

Hail! South Dakota, The state we love the best,
Land of our fathers, Builders of the west;
Home of the Badlands, and Rushmore's ageless shrine,
Black Hills and prairies, Farmland and Sunshine.
Hills, farms and prairies, Blessed with bright Sunshine.

NATURAL AREAS AND HISTORIC SITES

★ ★ ★

National Park

Badlands National Park features spectacular landscapes of eroded buttes, pinnacles, and spires.

Wind Cave National Park preserves one of the world's longest and most complex caves. The park also serves as a habitat for bison, elk, mule deer, and coyotes.

National Monument

Jewel Cave National Monument is the third-longest cave system in the world.

National Memorial

Mount Rushmore National Memorial shows the carved faces of George Washington, Thomas Jefferson, Theodore Roosevelt, and Abraham Lincoln.

National Recreational River

Meandering into South Dakota is the *Missouri National Recreational River*, which is a great place to see eagles, hawks, beavers, turtles, deer, and foxes.

National Historic Site

South Dakota's *Minuteman Missile National Historic Site* is home to a launch control facility and a missile silo complex.

National Historic Trail

Lewis & Clark National Historic Trail passes through South Dakota, following the route of Lewis and Clark's journey.

National Forest

South Dakota has one national forest, the *Black Hills National Forest*, which covers an area of more than 1.2 million acres (486,000 ha) and features Harney Peak, the tallest mountain in South Dakota and the highest peak east of the Rocky Mountains in the United States.

State Parks and Forests

South Dakota's state park system features and maintains 58 state park and recreation areas, including *Custer State Park*, *George S. Mickelson Trail*, and *Palisades State Park*.

SPORTS TEAMS

★ ★ ★

NCAA Teams (Division I)

Augustana College *Vikings*
Northern State University *Wolves*
South Dakota State University *Jackrabbits*
University of South Dakota *Coyotes*

A matchup between South Dakota State and North Dakota State men's basketball teams

CULTURAL INSTITUTIONS

Libraries

The *University of South Dakota Library* (Vermillion) and the South Dakota State University Library (Brookings) have the major academic collections in the state.

The *Sioux Falls Public Library* is the largest public library in the state, with special collections on art and the history of South Dakota.

The *Library of the South Dakota State Historical Society* holds extensive collections on the history of the state.

Museums

Museum of Geology at the South Dakota School of Mines and Technology (Rapid City) contains exhibits on the geology of South Dakota.

The *Sioux Indian Museum* (Rapid City) and the *W. H. Over Museum of Natural and Cultural History* (Vermillion) have collections related to American Indian heritage and history.

The *Cultural Heritage Center* (Pierre) contains displays of historical, military, and Indian artifacts that portray the life and culture of South Dakota from the days of the Plains Indians to modern times.

Performing Arts

The *Washington Pavilion of Arts and Science*, which opened in 1999 in Sioux Falls, presents top entertainers and world-class concerts.

Universities and Colleges

In 2006, South Dakota had 12 public and 11 private institutions of higher learning.

ANNUAL EVENTS

January–March

Black Hills Stock Show and Rodeo in Rapid City (February)

Schmeckfest in Freeman (late March/ early April)

April–June

Kids Fishing Day in Pierre (May)

Czech Days in Tabor (June)

Fort Sisseton Historical Festival in Fort Sisseton State Historical Park (June)

ICS Chili Cook-off in Belle Fourche (June)

Spring Arabian Horse Shows in Sioux Falls (June)

Laura Ingalls Wilder Pageant in De Smet (late June/early July)

July–September

Wall Celebration (July)

Black Hills Roundup in Belle Fourche (July)

Sitting Bull Stampede in Mobridge (July)

Gold Discovery Days in Custer (July)

Summer Arts Festival in Brookings (July)

Days of '76 Festival in Deadwood (July)

Selby Area Rodeo (August)

Lewis and Clark Sprint Triathlon in Chamberlain (August)

Sturgis Rally and Races (August)

Sioux Empire Fair in Sioux Falls (August)

Spearfish Motor Rally (August)

State Fair in Huron (late August/early September)

Mickelson Trail Ride in Lead (September)

Threshing Day in Dupree (September)

Corn Palace Festival in Mitchell (September)

Cheyenne River Sioux Tribe Fair, Rodeo, and Powwow in Eagle Butte (September)

Buffalo Roundup in Custer State Park (September/October)

October–December

Festival of Trees in Sioux Falls (November)

Parade of Lights in Pierre (November)

Capitol Christmas in Pierre (November/ December)

BIOGRAPHICAL DICTIONARY

George Lee "Sparky" Anderson (1934–), a native of Bridgewater, is one of the most successful baseball managers in history. His teams won three World Series, and he was elected to the National Baseball Hall of Fame.

Jesse Bail (1979–) is a rodeo star who excels at riding bulls and broncos—especially hard-to-ride horses. In 2000, he was the college all-around rodeo champion. He was born in Spearfish.

Bob Barker (1923–) spent most of his early life on South Dakota's Rosebud Reservation, where his mother was a teacher. He went on to become a TV star, hosting the game show *The Price Is Right* for 35 years.

Nicholas Black Elk (1863–1950), an Oglala Lakota medicine man and cousin of Crazy Horse, fought at the Battle of the Little Bighorn. He gave a series of interviews about his life and Sioux culture that became a best-selling book, *Black Elk Speaks*.

Gutzon Borglum (1867–1941) was born in Idaho and created a sculpture of Abraham Lincoln that now stands in the Capitol in Washington, D.C., before coming to South Dakota to begin his greatest work, Mount Rushmore. He had a team of workers who carried out his vision for carving the heads of four U.S. presidents out of rock.

Gutzon Borglum

Tom Brokaw (1940–), a TV journalist born in Webster, reported from the White House for NBC News and then served as the anchor for that network's nightly news broadcast.

Martha Jane Cannary (Calamity Jane) (c. 1852–1903) came to Deadwood when it was a booming gold town. She dressed as a man, worked as a scout, and adapted to the rough life on the frontier.

Pierre Chouteau Jr. (1789–1865), the son of a successful trader, followed in his father's footsteps. He built Fort Pierre, which gave its name to the nearby city, and brought the first steamboat up the Missouri River to South Dakota.

Amanda Clement See page 81.

Crazy Horse (1849–1877) was one of the bravest Sioux leaders. He fought hard to keep settlers out of Lakota lands and to preserve the traditional Sioux way of life.

Ella Deloria See page 29.

Tom Brokaw

Vine Deloria Jr. (1933–2005) was a writer and teacher who spoke out strongly for Indian rights and, for a time, led the National Congress of American Indians.

Pierre-Jean De Smet (1801–1873), a native of Belgium, was a priest who came to the United States in 1821 and arrived in South Dakota in 1839. During the 1860s, he spent time in the Badlands with the Lakota Nation, helping them maintain peaceful relations with European settlers.

Pete Dexter (1943–), a graduate of the University of South Dakota, was a reporter before becoming a prize-winning novelist. One of his earliest books explores the history of Deadwood.

Lawrence Diggs See page 106.

Harvey Dunn (1884–1952), who was born on a South Dakota homestead, was a painter and illustrator. Much of his work is now on display in South Dakota museums.

Charles Eastman (1858–1939) was a doctor who was part Santee Dakota. He wrote several books about his life as a Sioux and worked to improve the rights of all Native Americans.

Pete Dexter

Joe Foss See page 63.

Archer Gilfillan (1886–1955) spent almost two decades as a sheepherder in South Dakota and then wrote about his experiences in a best-selling book, *Sheep: Life on the South Dakota Range*.

Mary Hart (1950–), a former Miss South Dakota, has had a long career in TV, much of it as the co-host of *Entertainment Tonight*. She was born in Madison.

Linda M. Hasselstrom See page 21.

"Wild Bill" Hickok (1837–1876) was a sheriff and gunfighter who was killed in Deadwood while playing poker.

Oscar Howe See page 79.

Hubert Humphrey (1911–1978), a native of Wallace, later moved to Minnesota and entered politics. He served as the vice president of the United States from 1965 to 1969 and was the Democratic nominee for president in 1968.

Mary Hart

Abbie Jarvis (1854–1931) was South Dakota's first female doctor and helped deliver more than 600 babies.

Tim Johnson (1946–), a Canton native, has represented South Dakota in the U.S. Senate since 1997.

François de La Vérendrye (1715–1794) and **Louis-Joseph de La Vérendrye (1717–1761)** were the first Europeans known to have entered today's South Dakota. Two metal plates they left during their travels were discovered in the 20th century.

Ernest Lawrence See page 100.

Manuel Lisa See page 40.

George McGovern (1922–) was born in Avon, fought in World War II, and then became a U.S. representative, a U.S. senator, and the Democratic candidate for president in 1972. During his career, he stressed social and economic reforms and spoke out strongly against the Vietnam War.

Russell Means See page 66.

Billy Mills

Judith Meierhenry See page 89.

Oscar Micheaux See page 80.

Billy Mills (1938–) is an Oglala Lakota from the Pine Ridge Reservation. At the 1964 Olympics, he won a gold medal in the 10,000-meter race, becoming the first American to win the event.

Allen Neuharth (1924–) started his journalism career in South Dakota before becoming president of Gannett, a large newspaper company. There he created *USA Today*, the first national newspaper designed to cover general news across the country. He is from Eureka.

Richard Franklin Pettigrew (1848–1926) came to South Dakota to work for the U.S. government. He entered politics and in 1889 was elected one of South Dakota's first two U.S. senators. His home in Sioux Falls is open to the public.

Gladys Pyle (1890–1989), the daughter of Mamie Shields Pyle, was the first woman elected to the South Dakota legislature. She also briefly represented her home state by appointment in the U.S. Senate.

Mamie Shields Pyle See page 56.

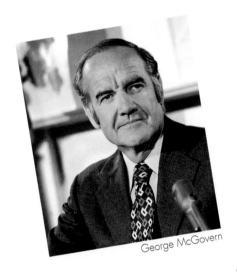
George McGovern

Red Cloud (1822–1909) was a Lakota leader who fought to keep white settlers off Sioux lands for several years. In 1876, he chose not to fight, arguing instead that Native Americans should have more control of reservations.

Ben Reifel See page 90.

O. E. Rolvaag (1876–1931), a Norwegian immigrant, was one of the first U.S. writers to use South Dakota as a setting for his novels. His most notable work is *Giants in the Earth: A Saga of the Prairie.*

T. Denny Sanford See page 101.

Sitting Bull See page 48.

Virginia Driving Hawk Sneve (1933–), a Lakota Sioux author, has written books for both children and adults. Her works include *Enduring Wisdom: Sayings from Native Americans.*

Casey Tibbs (1929–1990), who was born in a log cabin near Fort Pierre, became the first great professional rodeo champion, winning the national title for riding a bronco with a saddle six years in a row.

John Blair Smith Todd See page 42.

Adam Vinatieri

Adam Vinatieri (1972–) is a professional football player who was born in Yankton. He became a kicker for the South Dakota State University football team and then moved on to the National Football League.

Laura Ingalls Wilder See page 78.

Fee Lee Wong See page 50.

York See page 38.

Korczak Ziolkowski (1908–1982) was an artist who won a prize for a sculpture at the 1939 World's Fair and then received an invitation to come to the Black Hills and carve an image of the Lakota leader Crazy Horse out of rock. He spent the second half of his life in South Dakota.

Zitkala-Sa (Gertrude Simmons Bonnin) (1876–1938), the daughter of a white father and Sioux mother, was a writer whose books focus on Indian legends and stories as well as her experiences as a Native American.

Zitkala-Sa

RESOURCES

BOOKS

Nonfiction

Bodden, Valerie. *Mount Rushmore*. Mankato, Minn.: Creative Education, 2006.

Ditchfield, Christin. *The Lewis and Clark Expedition*. New York: Children's Press, 2006.

Englar, Mary. *The Sioux and Their History*. Minneapolis: Compass Point Books, 2006.

Harrison, Peter. *The Amazing World of the Wild West*. London: Lorenz, 2004.

Hasselstrom, Linda. *Feels Like Far: A Rancher's Life on the Great Plains*. New York: Lyons Press, 1999.

Hoover, Herbert T., et al. *A New South Dakota History*. Sioux Falls, S.D.: Center for Western Studies, 2005.

Landau, Elaine. *The Wounded Knee Massacre*. New York: Children's Press, 2004.

McLeese, Don. *Sitting Bull*. Vero Beach, Fla.: Rourke Publishing, 2004.

VanEpps-Taylor, Betti. *Forgotten Lives: African Americans in South Dakota*. Pierre: South Dakota State Historical Society Press, 2008.

Fiction

Arrington, Frances. *Prairie Whispers*. New York: Puffin Books, 2005.

Sneve, Virginia Driving Hawk. *Enduring Wisdom: Sayings from Native Americans*. New York: Holiday House, 2003.

Sneve, Virginia Driving Hawk. *Jimmy Yellow Hawk*. New York: Holiday House, 1977.

Wilder, Laura Ingalls. *The First Four Years*. New York: HarperTrophy, 2007.

Wilder, Laura Ingalls. *Little House on the Prairie*. New York: Harper, 1953.

DVDs

Bury My Heart at Wounded Knee. HBO Video, 2007.

Crazy Horse: The Last Warrior. A&E, 2005.

Dances with Wolves. Orion Home Video, 1998.

Modern Marvels: Mount Rushmore. History Channel, 2005.

Mt. Rushmore, Crazy Horse & the Black Hills. Finley-Holiday Film Corporation, 2001.

WEB SITES AND ORGANIZATIONS

Argus Leader Media

www.argusleader.com/apps/pbcs.dll/ frontpage
The online version of South Dakota's largest newspaper has the latest state and local news.

Atka Lakota Museum & Cultural Center

www.aktalakota.org/index.cfm?cat=1
For detailed information on Lakota life and history.

Deadwood Magazine

www.deadwoodmagazine.com
The online version of this magazine is filled with articles about the history of Deadwood and the Black Hills.

Discovering Lewis & Clark

www.lewis-clark.org
A detailed look at the entire Lewis and Clark expedition, including its time in South Dakota.

Lakota Mall

www.lakotamall.com
Based at the Pine Ridge Reservation, this site has links to Lakota companies and organizations, including the *Lakota Times*, a tribal newspaper.

Mount Rushmore National Memorial

www.nps.gov/moru
The National Park Service Web site for South Dakota's most famous tourist attraction has the history of the site and a visitor guide that you can print before traveling to the memorial.

New Perspectives on the West

www.pbs.org/weta/thewest/people
Based on a PBS television series, this Web site has information on many people and events from South Dakota's history.

South Dakota State Historical Society

www.sdhistory.org
Learn more about South Dakota history with online exhibits, including the full text of important state documents.

South Dakota State Library

http://library.sd.gov/sdfacts
For facts of all kinds about South Dakota and its people.

State of South Dakota

www.sd.gov
The official state Web site has the latest news on government policies and programs and links to even more information.

Travel SD

www.travelsd.com
This is the state's main online source for tourist information. Whether you want to explore cities, the Black Hills, or Sioux reservations, this is a great starting point.

INDEX

★ ★ ★

AUTHOR'S TIPS AND SOURCE NOTES

★ ★ ★

I read many books while doing research for this book. Particularly helpful was *A New South Dakota History*, which features chapters by a variety of South Dakota writers as well as scholars from nearby states. Herbert Schell wrote a detailed history of the state, *History of South Dakota*, which was updated by John E. Miller. To understand South Dakota's geography, I turned to *The Geography of South Dakota* by Edward Patrick Hogan and Erin Hogan Fouberg. Guy Gibbon's *The Sioux* gives both historical and recent information on the Lakota, Nakota, and Dakota Sioux. And *South Dakota*, written by state resident T. D. Griffith, provided useful information on events and sites throughout the state. The state of South Dakota's Web site and the sites for two newspapers, the *Argus Leader* and the *Rapid City Journal*, were essential for information on the state government, economy, and current affairs.